Below Your Belt

How To Be Queen *of* Your Pelvic Region

Missy Lavender
Jeni Donatelli Ihm

Illustrations by Jan Dolby

"*Below Your Belt* is weirdly awesome!"
> – 13-year old, Mercy Home, Chicago, Illinois

"I didn't know all this stuff, and now I do the 'Rock and Roll'. It really works!"
> – Aurora, 14

"I think it's really helpful because a lot of girls don't know what's going on about their body. It's nice to be 'in the know' and have good information. I am proud of my mother!" (Missy)
> – Fallon, 14

"This book was really helpful explaining things that I've always wondered, like how girls and women dealt with their periods in ancient times. I thought it might be too embarrassing to google, so I never knew the answer until reading this."
> – Caroline, 13

"I like the fun, creative exercises and didn't know my pelvis could make me more powerful."
> – Lily, 12

An amazing new book has arrived. It challenges one of the most controversial parts of our public, private and homeschool curriculum. It goes up against traditions of silence and misinformation. And I love it. Women's Health Foundation has produced a lovely, age appropriate book for young girls. This book is written to dispel myths, quiet fears and generate conversations. And it is a success. It is written to teach the truth about pelvic health for girls.

    Below Your Belt covers peeing, pooping, periods and exercise. It addresses how great it is to be female. No shame, just honest discussion and cleverly delivered information. As a pelvic health physical therapist I am particular about the information surrounding bowel, bladder and pelvic muscle function. I look forward to sharing this book in our clinic library and recommending it to patients, friends and family.
> – Sandra Hilton, PT, DPT, MS
> Co-Author, *Why Pelvic Pain Hurts*

Below Your Belt is a great book and should be in the hands of every girl on planet Earth! Bravo , Bravo, Bravo!!"
— Christiane Northrup, M.D.
OBGYN, physician, and author of the New York Times bestsellers: *Goddesses Never Age: The Secret Prescription for Radiance, Vitality, and Wellbeing; Women's Bodies, Women's Wisdom; The Wisdom of Menopause, and Mother-Daughter Wisdom: Understanding the Crucial Link Between Mothers, Daughters, and Health*

The work you did is fabulous!! I am so impressed. The stats related to the lack of correct body, menstrual, and pelvic information is overwhelming so the information you offer is awesome. Your work is long overdue. Congratulations!!!
— Francie Bernier, Ph.D., RN
Assistant Professor, Eleanor Wade Custer School of Nursing, Shenandoah University

I am SO EXCITED about this book. I think it is absolutely wonderful!!
— Jill Stein
Resource Coordinator, Northwestern Memorial Hospital, Osher Center for Integrative Medicine, Chicago, IL, Wellness Institute, Total Control™ Instructor

I think *Below Your Belt* is phenomenal! I love how it has such a focus on confidence-building and empowerment. The sections about reproductive health, specifically menstruation, are introduced in a way that is really separate from either sexual intimacy or motherhood. It retains an emphasis on young women's own identity development. I also love how BYB is focused on young women learning to take care of their own bodies for themselves.
— Elizabeth Jarpe-Ratner
School and Adolescent Health Researcher, University of Illinois at Chicago School of Public Health

I have loved reading *Below Your Belt*. The chapters flow so smoothly, and the information is presented in such an easily understood manner. I especially like the pages on the Princess of Ovulation! Charming and cute while imparting really important information. Job well done.

    – Kathy Pickus
      Founder, Dot Girl First Period Kits®

Below Your Belt is easy to read with fun facts, drawings and information. It explains needed information from bodily functions to exercise, from periods to stretching, from cramps to hygiene. This is a great read for all young girls (and their mothers) who are about to start on the road to becoming young ladies.

    – Joann V. Pinkerton, MD
      Professor of Obstetrics and Gynecology, Director Midlife
      Health University of Virginia Health Center

What a charming way to introduce girls not only to periods, but all other facets of their (ahemm), nether regions. Using a style that is both engaging and humorous, Missy and Jeni have written a book sure to pique the interest of many young girls.

    – Toni Weschler, MPH
      Author of *Cycle Savvy* and *Taking Charge of Your Fertility*

It is never too early to start teaching healthy habits - including those that affect us "below the belt"! This is a great book club book. Enjoy learning and sharing the information in "*Below Your Belt*".

    – Linda BrubakerMD, MS
      Dean and Chief Diversity Officer, Stritch School of Medicine,
      Loyola University Chicago

I wish I'd had this book 15 years ago when my own daughters were young. The illustrations are charming and fun, and the book makes important information approachable.

    – Dr. Barbara Depree, MD
      Director of Midlife Women's Health at Holland Hospital,
      Holland, MI, Founder, Middlesex MD

Below Your Belt: How to be Queen of Your Pelvic Region
Authors: Missy Lavender and Jeni Donatelli Ihm
Illustrator: Jan Dolby
Published by Women's Health Foundation, Chicago, Illinois

www.womenshealthfoundation.org
info@womenshealthfoundation.org

10 9 8 7 6 5 4 3 2 1

Printed in the USA

ISBN 13: 9780996535809

Editor: Elizabeth Wood, Women's Health Foundation
Design: Michelle Ganeles, Kym Abrams

The advice and strategies in *Below Your Belt: How to be Queen
of Your Pelvic Region* are general and may not be suitable in
all situations. The content should not be used as a substitute
for the advice of a doctor or medical professional.

WITH GRATITUDE . . .

First, we would like to thank Dr. Tamara Bavendam, a visionary who four years ago, believed in what we wanted to do - teach girls about their pelvic health and change the world. She helped us secure the funding to do the research that created our adolescent curriculum that informed this book. We are deeply grateful for Toni Weschler's inspiration and permission to translate for a younger audience, her definitive book, Cycle Savvy, in our ovulation and menstruation chapters. We'd like to thank all the girls who have given us their time, their spirit and their energy - in small groups, in the study, and in book discussions. We are grateful for everyone who worked on the research study and helped make WHF's Adolescent Pelvic Health Initiative a reality. Ditto for the dedicated Women's Health Foundation staff. You are all part of the final product, and we could not have done it without you.

Secondly, we would like to acknowledge our WHF team member and editor, Elizabeth Wood, for her tireless work crafting, detailing, and art directing the BYB message. She has given this project her all, both for every girl who reads it and for her own darling daughter. We thank also Jan Dolby, our fearless and imaginative illustrator, who turned every concept into an endearing rendering.

We dedicate this book to our daughters, Fallon and Sophia, who are growing up knowledgeable and strong in their bodies, because we have been sharing this amazing information with them - sometimes to their chagrin - for years. They have mothers whom some would call "Bladder Queens." We hope one day they can be proud of our work, just as we are so very proud of them. We also hope they and their friends can continue to help us change the way girls think about things below the belt, affirming pelvic health as a family value for future generations.

You go, girls!
Missy & Jeni

NOTE TO PARENTS

Dear Grown-ups,

When was the last time anyone talked to you about your bladder or bowels or anything "below the belt" - not related to giving birth? It probably has been awhile. Most likely, it was when you were about three and needing to be potty trained in order to go to preschool or swim without a diaper.

Sadly, for most girls, that's when training or communication about pelvic health ends. Usually after these milestones are reached, there is no recognition that a pelvis is even part of the body. We are left to our own devices to figure out critical things like the proper way to go to the bathroom (dare we say "poop" and "pee"?) or how to keep things clean "down there." Maybe our mothers told us about their periods; then again, maybe not. Basically, girls all over the world are left to make it up as they encounter each new experience. In doing so, they run the risk of jeopardizing their overall health, specifically their pelvic health.

It's hard to comprehend that behavior now can have any effect at all down the road. Many grown women assume that pelvic pain, organ prolapse, and the repercussions of bladder leakage are just a normal part of womanhood and aging. They are not. Teaching good pelvic health practices now can lead to enhanced pelvic wellness later.

We say enough is enough! It is time for all of us moms (and dads) to help our young girls learn about this wonderful and powerful place called the Pelvic Region. We want to help them understand all the "what's" and "why's" of healthy bathroom behaviors, about their periods, and the proper care of their delicate body parts before they are introduced to the wonders and complexities of sexuality. You could think of *Below Your Belt* as a foundation or stepping stone into this topic that many parents, organizations, books, and websites teach beautifully.

Based on our research, the guidelines and suggestions in this book can change the way girls feel about their own bodies and how they perceive themselves as young women in today's environment. We want to positively feed and nurture a sense of connection and pride, as well as create an entire generation of girls and women who both know and love and take care of all things below the belt. We believe this is powerful and important, and we are SO very glad you decided to buy *Below Your Belt* for your daughter or a young girl in your charge.

Please take the opportunity to read it yourself or share it with her out loud. After that, she may want to keep it in her room as a reference, as her body changes or as she encounters "stuff" or has questions. When she becomes satisfied with what she has learned, please pay it forward and give our book to another young girl like her.

From the beginning of time, women have shared their wisdom with the next generation. As sisters in pelvic health, we all can do the same.

Enjoy, and happy reading!

Missy Lavender

Missy Lavender

NOTE TO GIRLS

Dear Wonderful You!

E very week you probably learn something about your health, your periods, and your changing body, and there is a very important part of you that has been mostly overlooked. That's because no one really looks at or thinks about the whole big picture **BELOW YOUR BELT**. This book is going to teach you about the seldom talked about part of the body known as your **PELVIS**: what it is, what's inside it, what it does, and how to keep it strong and healthy over the course of your life. By the end of this book, you will know so much about your **PELVIC REGION** you may as well be **QUEEN** of it!

It's ok to **LOL** while you read **BYB**. The truth is not many people will talk to you at all about what's in this book. That's why we wrote it. We want you to know all about you and why you are so special – you're a girl! We want you to know how important and amazing this part of your body is, how it functions, and how to treasure it and take good care of it – so you can continue to grow and develop with a new sense of ownership and understanding.

Go ahead, turn the page and discover the world below your belt. Power to the Pelvis!

With admiration,

Jeni Ihm

TABLE OF CONTENTS

CHAPTER ONE:
It's About Time!

RIGHT THIS VERY MINUTE

You might be wondering, "Queen of my what?!" or "Why does my pelvis even matter?" While you may have guessed that having periods and having babies are a part of pelvic health, and you would be correct, did you know that using the bathroom or performing well in sports is also about pelvic health? Your whole pelvic region — everything below your belt — is where the big stuff in life happens!

Let's look at it this way:

**YOU HAVE BEEN PEEING
OR POOPING**
from the moment you were
born and using the bathroom
by yourself since you were
about three years old. Peeing
and pooping are about bladder
and bowel health, which are
both part of pelvic health.

**IF YOU HAVEN'T GOTTEN
YOUR PERIOD YET**
you are likely just about to start.
The purpose of menstruation,
dealing with cramps or PMS,
and what to do in sports while
you have your period, are all
part of pelvic health.

*Learn about your
pelvic region now,
and you will rock
& rule your pelvic
health through life!*

WHETHER BALLET OR SOCCER

you know how important it is to be strong and fit. Well, if you don't know about the special muscles of your pelvis, you will miss out on a wonderful secret to winning!

WHY IS THIS CHAPTER CALLED "IT'S ABOUT TIME?"

Because until now, there hasn't been ANY book about pelvic health for girls! There have been books about periods all right, but no books that talk about the big pelvic picture.

The Past

Speaking of periods, let's go back in time way before you were born: Have you ever wondered how they did it? Before we had the comfort of private indoor bathrooms, pads that stay in place – pads with wings! Or more than one pair of underwear. Even running water from a faucet. How *did* they do it?

They had each other – girls helping girls, mothers helping daughters, sisters helping sisters, aunties helping nieces, grandmothers helping granddaughters – you get the picture. Each one of these wise women learned from the woman who came before her, and so on and so on. Well, take that chain of girls and women all the way back to centuries and decades ago…

Rags, reeds, leaves, metal, cotton, wool, and nothing! Which one of these things do you think women used when they had their periods? Can you believe all of them have been used to keep things "clean" during that time of the month?

Even in the 1970s, which wasn't that long ago, women didn't have the teeny pads and tampons you find in stores now. Can you say belts and snaps? That's true! Whether you were a hippie or a doctor, you would wear a special belt to fit under your underwear with snaps in the front and the back to connect a pad to it. Awkward to say the least and about a thousand times better than what came before that!

Let's take a walk through history and discover the funky ways people thought about pelvic health:

CONSTIPATION IN THE 1600s

In 1609, an English surgeon, John Woodall, made a new instrument to treat constipation. It looked like a 12-inch-long spatula and was called the "Spatula Mundani," which kind of sounds like a pasta dish! The spoon end of the spatula was used to remove hard poops from inside the body while the other end was used to mix medicine and apply ointments. Ew.

BATHROOMS IN THE 1700s

Privacy was a bit of an issue, and we all know when you don't have privacy it makes it kind of hard to do your "business." Running water in every house just wasn't available. So, imagine your whole family taking a trip to the public outhouse where there were enough toilet seats for everyone! If you wanted some privacy, you had to "rent" a cloak and a bucket so you could cover yourself while going to the bathroom in the bucket... on the street. Seriously!

NUTRITION IN THE 1900s

Every day it seems like someone is chirping in your ear about healthy eating, but people really didn't think about everyday nutrition until about 1900. Scientists and doctors finally started to realize the benefits of a balanced diet. People actually saw a difference in their health by changing what they ate. Also, in the early 1900s, schools started providing lunches for their students. Share that with your lunch lady!

PERIODS IN THE 1800s

In the late 1890s, an English woman named Selina Cooper devoted herself to helping women she saw on the farm where she worked. Other women who worked on the farm did not use any sort of sanitary protection when they menstruated. Instead, the women let their period blood flow! Each month, their coats and dresses had blood stains, and the farm floors were covered in straw to collect the blood. Selina introduced them to the first "pads" which were similar to rolled up towels placed in women's underwear.

Just a little bulky, don't you think?

PREGNANCY IN THE 1950s

Just like now, pregnant women were given pamphlets of information by their doctor. It was a little different, though! Not that long ago, doctors told pregnant women they should not watch football or hockey because these sports were too exciting for an unborn baby. Now maybe someone wouldn't play football or hockey if pregnant, but watch? We now know that's ok.

GOOD NEWS IN THE 1970s

Have you ever heard of an ADVOCATE (AD-vo-cat)? An advocate is a person who stands up for children, for animals, for the well-being of people in less fortunate countries than our own, and many other causes. Well, in the 1970s advocates for women's health worked very hard to make sure all women felt comfortable going to their doctors for help and that they received the care they needed, regardless of their race, or how much money they made, or where they lived. These advocates taught women to take charge of their own health. Now that's girl power!

FITNESS IN THE 1990s

While everyone knows that exercise and fitness are good things, it really wasn't until the early '90s that doctors and women's health advocates began to see that exercise wasn't just "good for you," it could actually improve health. Now we know that targeted exercise for different areas of your body, like pelvic exercise, creates strength, balance, flexibility, and great health overall. See how that works?

Take note! Any exercise is better than no exercise, so find some ways to move that make you happy, and go for it!

THROUGH THE AGES

Belly dancing originated in the Middle East and goes back centuries. It was – and still is today – a wonderful form of expression. Originally, belly dancing was performed by women for other women in a private setting so they could feel comfortable moving their bodies to show their feelings. Now there are belly dancing classes and performances all over the world because it's fun to watch, and it's a good way to strengthen stomach muscles!

The Present

THREE NEW WORDS FOR YOU!

Scandalous (SCAN-duh-lus): shocking or offensive

Norm (norm): usual or expected

Taboo (tab-BOO): an experience or subject people might find uncomfortable or unacceptable to talk about

Way before Beyoncé and Shakira, there were many hot pop stars, both guys and girls. Some of these "hip" cats danced and moved in such a way that was thought to be **SCANDALOUS** by many people. Teenagers went bonkers for all that new dancing. One scandalous pop star of note was actually a dude. You may have heard of him: Elvis Presley, also known as Elvis the Pelvis. Elvis had total swag. Back in the '50s no one had ever seen moves like his! He opened the door for all the other performers who have followed in his footsteps. More recent pop stars and heart throbs have raised the bar a bit – meaning they do things on stage Elvis wouldn't have dreamed of doing.

Eventually people got used to Elvis' crazy gyrations, and each generation since has become a little more comfortable with the latest pop star's moves – which now makes all this hip action the **NORM**! (Get it? 'Hip' as in groovy and 'hip' as in bones?) Movement isn't only good for your health, it can also be a wonderful way to express feelings and creativity as well as explore many different cultures. Remember the belly dancers?

Connecting the Dots

Lots of things in life which were once **TABOO** are now the **NORM** and no longer **SCANDALOUS**.

MOTHER'S thoughts...

1960s
NOT OK

1980s
INTERESTING

2000s
OK

A great example of this **SCANDALOUS** concept is what you will be learning in this book and hopefully discussing with your friends and family. It's ok to talk about all aspects of your pelvic region including poop and pee – not just the period parts. These subjects have been **TABOO**, but we're here to talk about them a lot until they become the **NORM**. We're making history here, girls!

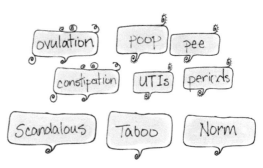

ovulation   poop   pee
constipation   UTIs   periods
Scandalous   Taboo   Norm

LEARN ABOUT YOUR BODY NOW WHILE YOU ARE YOUNG

You know that as young girls grow and become women, changes happen "down there." The information in this book may help you treat your pelvic region with more interest and not shove it to the side and disconnect from it, as many grown women do.

AS YOU GET TO KNOW YOUR PELVIC REGION

what makes you a girl, and how to keep your body healthy, you can help other girls, too! You know how when you smile at people they smile back? The same thing happens with health. When you are actively healthy, you motivate others to be healthy, too, as they watch and learn from you.

Now that's exactly what a Queen would do!

The next chapters will take you on a journey. Hold on tight because you are in for an exciting ride all around your pelvic region!

CHAPTER TWO

Welcome to Your Pelvis

WHAT EXACTLY IS YOUR PELVIS?

Is it where your belly button is? Is it part of your bum? Or is it just where your private parts are? Actually, it's all of it. Your pelvis is a wonderful and mysterious place. Welcome!

YOUR PELVIC REGION

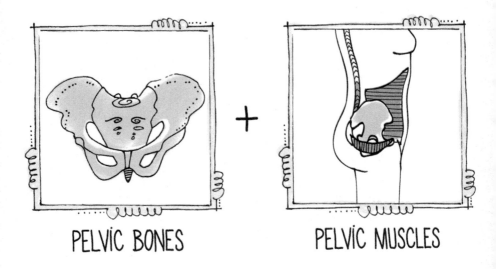

PELVIC BONES + PELVIC MUSCLES

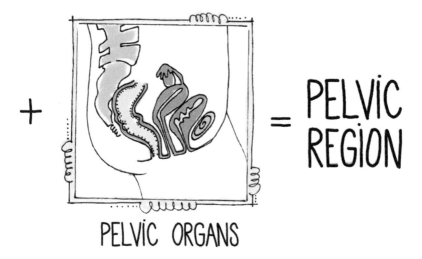

+ PELVIC ORGANS = PELVIC REGION

THE ORGANS OF THE PELVIC REGION support totally different systems, like your urinary system (pee), your digestive and elimination systems (poop), your reproductive system (for right now, your periods), certain special organs that make you unique and beautiful – a girl for that matter – and a group of muscles that help hold them all together.

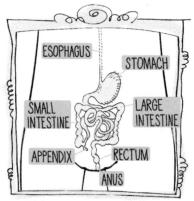

DIGESTIVE SYSTEM

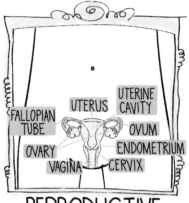

REPRODUCTIVE SYSTEM

GETTING TO KNOW ALL THE PARTS

hard ones, soft ones, and muscle-y ones, can keep you "connected" to your pelvis throughout your life, instead of pretending it's not even there – until, that is, you *have* to pay attention because something in your pelvic region isn't working so well.

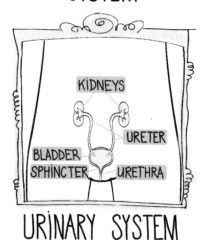

URINARY SYSTEM

19

When you look at this image of the pelvis, what do you see?

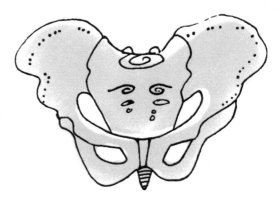

SOME PEOPLE see a butterfly. We think the big bones of the pelvis look like they come together to create a space, like a bowl or a basket.

ALL THE GOODIES in and around this bowl are called organs. If you imagine turning the basket to the side, can you see how nicely they fit into the pelvic bones?

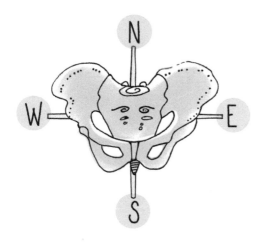

**MOST OF YOUR
PELVIC PARTS**
are inside of you. Some of them are outside of you, too. To the north you've got your intestines, to the south you've got some other wonderful stuff, all treasures.

**BY THE END OF
THIS CHAPTER**
you'll really know the geography of your pelvic region and be proud to call it your own. Let's see what's going on down there. Be sure to look at the different maps of your pelvis as we take our tour. Wear your hiking boots. Bring some water!

Protective Parts – Bones, Muscles, and Padding

The protective parts of your pelvis are like walls, barriers, and cushions, holding and protecting the organs inside them.

Know Your Bones

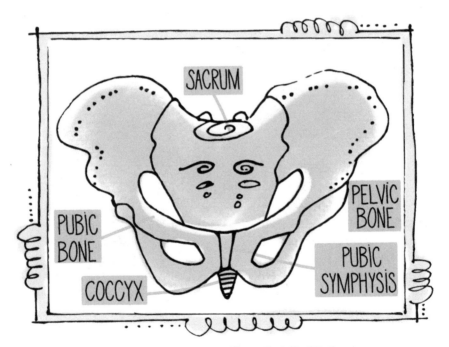

PROTECTIVE PARTS: BONES

LET'S LOOK AT THE BONES THAT MAKE THAT BUTTERFLY SHAPE

Technically, you have **TWO PELVIC BONES** – one on the left and one on the right. You can see that they kind of wrap around to the front becoming much narrower. These bones in front are called your **PUBIC BONES**. They are held together by a strip of cartilage called the **PUBIC SYMPHYSIS (SYM-fuh-sis)**. Not symphony. (What's cartilage you ask? Cartilage is softer than bone and harder than muscle and is attached to certain bones and joints in your body that move around as *you* move around. Knees, for instance. Also, ears.)

Your pelvic bones are held together in the back by a funny, flatish bone called the **SACRUM (Say-crum)**. Attached to the top of the sacrum is the base or beginning of your spine, which goes all the way up to the base of your noggin, AKA skull.

At the bottom of the sacrum is your tail bone with the weird and hard-to-pronounce name, **COCCYX (COX-icks)**. You may not even realize you have a tail bone unless you have fallen on your fanny. It can hurt! Well, your tail bone is doing its job to protect the organs inside your pelvis if you do happen to fall.

Muscle Memory

Your body is wrapped tightly from head to toe with all kinds of muscles, just under your skin and deep inside your body. The muscles of your pelvis are **VERY DEEP** inside of you. You can't see them if you try to flex them, like you can see your biceps when you curl up your arms. The cool thing is if you learn where they are and how they feel, and you remember to engage them before you do any kind of physical activity, you can totally **ROCK AND RULE YOUR PELVIC REGION** your whole life long.

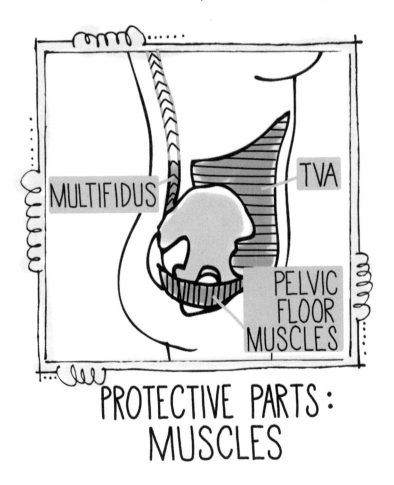

PROTECTIVE PARTS:
MUSCLES

YOUR PELVIC MUSCLES ARE WOVEN
in and around your spine and pelvic bones creating that "basket" we talk about. Take a look at drawing on the left.

The gray space you see in the middle is one of the two pelvic bones.

There are three big muscles of the pelvic region. We refer to them as the Pelvic Pyramid. The two most important, right now, while you are young:

TRANSVERSE ABDOMINAL (TVA) which is deep inside and wraps around your torso.

and

MULTIFIDUS (Mul-TI-fid-us) which runs deep inside along your spine.

A little later, we'll show you how to kick farther, spin faster, and stand taller than ever, just by engaging these super-secret muscles.

Adding Padding

Remember the narrow pubic bones that wrap around the front of your pelvic framework? These lucky bones have their very own kind of protection. Take a look at yourself in a full length mirror. The area on the outside of your body, on the lowest part of your torso, just below your bikini line, right in the center, is called the **MONS PUBIS** (sounds like **monz pyoobis**). If you press on it, you will find it's a little bit padded or fleshy – like a cushion. Your mons pubis helps make a fall onto your front side, on your pubic bones, a little softer, while keeping the delicate organs just under them a little more protected.

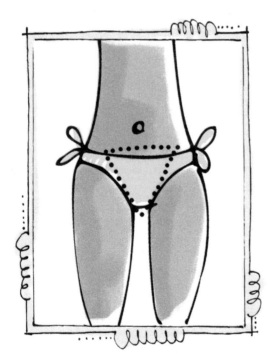

And, you thought this was just a blank space on your bod with no name.

PROTECTIVE PADDING

ROYAL WORDS OF WISDOM

"Our bodies are a special thing for us, and I think we should know about them and what things we can do."

"I want to share the information because I think it's good for girls to know what's wrong and what's right."

"Now that I know, I'll be more conscious."

– Comments from some of the girls who participated in Below Your Belt discussions.

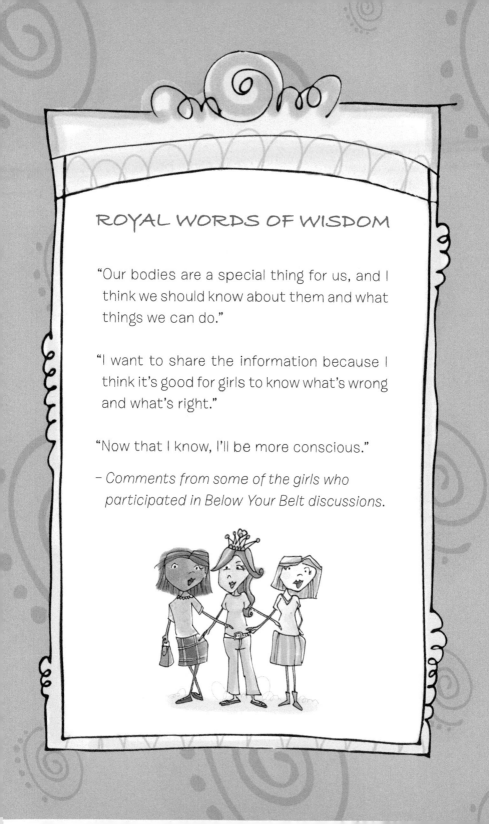

Digestive Parts – Your Guts

DIGESTION IS

the process of breaking down food by mechanical and enzymatic action into substances that can be used by the body. Blah. Blah. Blah!

Your body digests the food you eat from your first bite of breakfast, all day, and long into the night. You EAT IT. You CHEW IT. You SWALLOW IT, and little bitty microscopic proteins called ENZYMES start to break it all down. The good stuff – the vitamins, minerals, and fiber - makes its way into your blood stream and digestive tract. That's "tract" not "track."

Read on.....

The thing to know about digestion is this:

ONCE FOOD ENTERS YOUR MOUTH
it travels from there through your esophagus, and into your stomach. From there it passes into your intestines – located where? In your pelvic region!

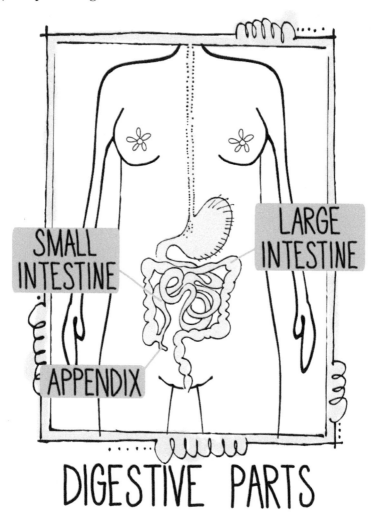

DIGESTIVE PARTS

Partially digested food flows from your stomach into your long and loopy **small intestine** first, and then on into your **large intestine.**

THE SMALL ONE

is connected to your stomach and ends up all nice and snug in the bowl created by your pelvic bones, wrapping around and around and back and forth like a big bowl of spaghetti. The small intestine moves partly digested food from your stomach to your large intestine, becoming liquidy along the way. Your small intestine is looooong! Take 20 regular-size steps, and that's about right. Seriously.

THE LARGE ONE

is large not because it is longer - it's actually much, much shorter than the small intestine. It's bigger around though, and it frames the small intestine, eventually heading toward your rectum and anus. What is left of any earlier eaten food has solidified and has become poop by this point.

COLON is another name for large intestine.

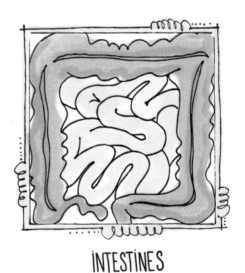

INTESTINES

WHEN FOOD DOESN'T DIGEST WELL

it can slow things down and get backed up. That leads to **CONSTIPATION.** It can also feel just awful if food moves through your intestines too quickly. Ever had **DIARRHEA?**

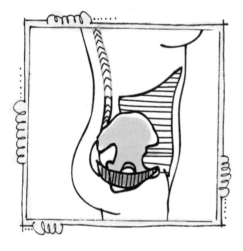

WE'LL COVER CONSTIPATION

later on because it can be hard on the muscles of your pelvic region. The good news is that there are lots of ways to help keep the food you eat right on track and out of the station on time.

YOU HAVE A BONUS DIGESTIVE ORGAN

known as your **APPENDIX**. It's an odd little pocket between your small and large intestines. It is believed that a million years ago, it held on to things that digested really slowly – like tree bark. Many scientists believe that the appendix has no purpose, but more recent research suggests that your appendix holds valuable, healthy bacteria which jump into action when you have an infection in your digestive tract. Cool!

Elimination Parts –
Out with the Old

YOUR FANTASTIC PELVIC REGION
CLEARS OUT YOUR OLD STUFF

and makes room for new stuff, the process known as **ELIMINATION**. Also known as **PEEING** and **POOPING.**

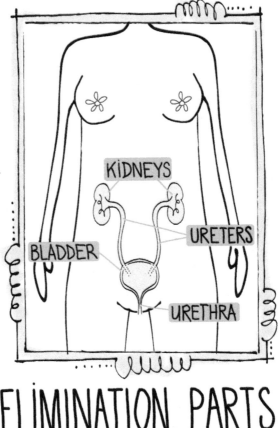

ELIMINATION PARTS

As pelvic region queens ourselves, we talk about these two lovely activities a lot. Stay tuned for upcoming chapters! For the moment, we just want you to know where these parts are and what they do.

Let's take a look:

KIDNEYS Like two little factories working around the clock, your kidneys sit just above your pelvis and are protected by your ribcage. They filter out waste from your blood, which then exits your fine bod in the form of urine.

URETERS are the thick tubes that take this urine from your kidneys to your bladder.

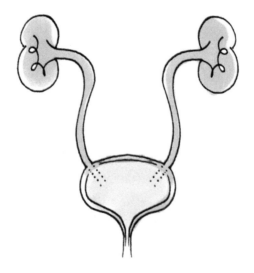

Just like the old song goes, some people say,

and others say...

poe-TAY-toe   your-REE-terz
poe-TAH-toe   your-reh-terz

BLADDER Your bladder, actually a muscle, is like a balloon or plastic baggie that expands and holds urine inside until you are ready to pee.

URETHRA Now, don't get ureters mixed up with urethras. Once you feel the need to pee, and you have seated yourself on the pot (or the bushes if you happen to be on a long drive with your parents and there's no bathroom for a hundred miles), you relax. Urine flows from your bladder through your urethra. The urethra is considered both an inside part and an outside part of the region because it starts inside and ends as an opening to the great outdoors.

RECTUM You just read about your large intestine, or colon. Here's the rest of that story: Once waste hits the end of your large intestine, it enters your rectum and stays there until you feel you are ready to poop.

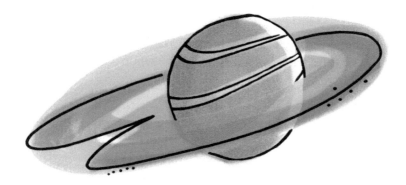

ANUS Yes, we know it sounds like the planet. Your anus is the opening that carries waste from your rectum to your toilet.

It can take anywhere from a couple of hours to several days for food to pass from your stomach to the very end of the tract . . . the toilet!

YOU MAY HAVE THOUGHT THE QUEEN of her pelvic region was all sparkles and glamour until you read about digestion and elimination. Well, some folks really do believe the way each part of your body has a very specific job to do, and usually does it really well, is indeed pretty glamorous.

Reproductive Parts – Your Gift!

Our very special reproductive parts are what make
us girls and give us a unique and powerful gift:
the ability to carry a new life into the world!

The system in your pelvic region in charge of all that is officially
known as **REPRODUCTION**. It works one way when women and
girls have their periods, and another way when a woman becomes
pregnant.

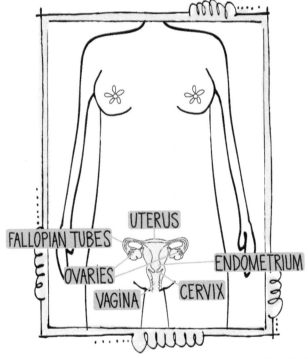

FALLOPIAN TUBES

UTERUS

OVARIES

ENDOMETRIUM

VAGINA

CERVIX

REPRODUCTIVE PARTS

Something truly incredible about your pelvis is its **SYMMETRY** –
what appears on one side also appears as a mirror image on the
other side. This is especially true when you look at the **OVARIES**
and **FALLOPIAN TUBES**.

Check it out:

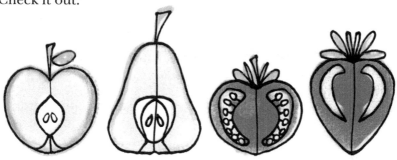

OVARIES Two almond-sized "purses" or **GLANDS** containing at least a million teeny tiny eggs from the first day of your life.

FALLOPIAN TUBES An egg from either ovary will travel through these, into your **UTERUS**, each month.

UTERUS A pear-shaped muscular organ where a baby grows for nine months. It's hard to imagine that a uterus is only the size of a fist until it stretches to hold a growing baby. When pregnant, a woman's uterus is commonly referred to as her "womb" (woom).

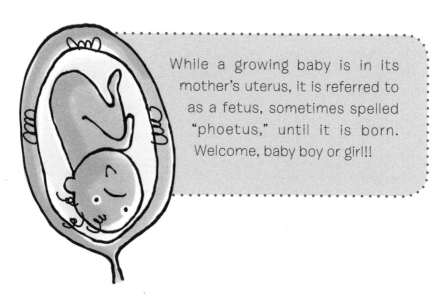

While a growing baby is in its mother's uterus, it is referred to as a fetus, sometimes spelled "phoetus," until it is born. Welcome, baby boy or girl!!

ENDOMETRIUM This is the lining inside the uterus which comes loose and sheds each month when you menstruate or provides nourishment for a growing baby.

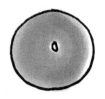

CERVIX A portal that connects your uterus to your vagina. The doughnut-shaped opening expands when it's time for a baby's delivery.

VAGINA A muscular passageway for the flow of menstrual blood on the way out of your body, and the birth canal for the delivery of a baby as it makes its way into the world.

honey pot tutu
va-jj POWDER
COOCHIE PUFF

What do *you* call it down there? Come on now, we know you have a name for it! Some are family names passed down through generations, and some are just made up. The real name? Vagina.

URETHRA-VAGINA-ANUS CONNECTION

TRUE OR FALSE:

I have only two openings in my pelvis. The one I pee from and the one I poop from.

ANSWER:

If you are a boy, this is true. If you are a girl, you have three openings down there! Can you name them?* Do you know which is which?

*Hint: Check out the title of this box!

Other Parts in the Region – Mi'lady Parts

While all your pelvic parts are private – because they are yours - the area we are about to discover is *especially* private. Your pelvic region includes delicate and sensitive territory! The parts in and around your vagina.

Let's have a quick discussion about boys: Unlike boys, we can't really see our private parts without looking for them. Boys know their own really well. How can they not? Their penis and other parts are on the outside of their body. Girls' private parts are more of a mystery.

Our friend, **Toni Weschler**, wrote a wonderful book for older girls, called *Cycle Savvy* (not exactly about bicycles). She says,

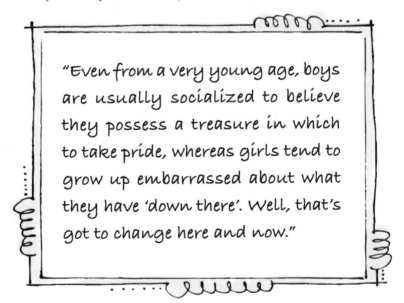

"Even from a very young age, boys are usually socialized to believe they possess a treasure in which to take pride, whereas girls tend to grow up embarrassed about what they have 'down there'. Well, that's got to change here and now."

We totally agree! It's one of the reasons we have written *Below Your Belt!*

PRIVATE PARTS, WHETHER THEY'RE GIRLS' OR BOYS'
are technically known as **GENITALIA (jen-ih-TAIL-ya).** You may
hear people refer to this area, as well as your reproductive parts,
as your **SEXUAL ORGANS** once you've hit puberty. They are
important and beautiful. Be confident, not embarrassed! Your
body is fascinating, and so worth getting to know; and the more
you know about your body, the more you will take care of it!

Your Personal Flower Power

**HAVE YOU EVER
LOOKED CLOSELY AT A FLOWER?**
We mean really looked at it, opened its petals, felt how soft it was,
and admired its beauty? Or seen that each daisy or each rose or
tulip is not exactly like its neighbor in the garden? There's no
shame in examining flowers, right? Well, your genitalia are often
compared to a flower. There is something so amazing about the
whole area when you really look. And, hear this: There is *no shame*
in looking, examining, touching, and learning.

A Private Tour of Your Private Parts

IF YOU ARE COMFORTABLE WITH THE IDEA

we are going to ask you to get out a hand mirror or situate yourself in front of a larger mirror so you can really see and examine your mi'lady parts. You will need a **PRIVATE**, well-lighted place where you can be by yourself in a secure area and take time to see what's really going on – where things are and what they feel like. There is no right or wrong way to do this. No worries if you don't want to explore either, just read along and maybe in the future you will feel more comfortable looking around.

A QUICK NOTE HERE

It's ok to discuss this tour with your mom or another trusted girl or woman in your life, or your doctor, before or after you have taken a look. It might be really helpful to ask questions or share your thoughts and feelings about the experience.

VULVA Sounds like a certain Swedish car, but there's no steering wheel here! Your vulva is the whole area surrounding your vagina, extending up to your mons pubis. Really, the words genitalia and vulva refer to the same parts. Another way to think of it is that your vulva is everything you can see by just looking in the mirror, and that your vulva is an area, not a particular "thing" like an organ or a muscle. Included in this area are the parts we'll look at next.

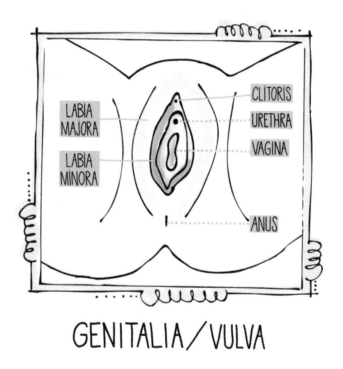

GENITALIA/VULVA

LABIA MAJORA Like the outer petals of a flower, the skin right around the opening of your vagina is also referred to as outer vaginal lips. Pubic hair can grow here once puberty starts.

LABIA MINORA These are known as inner vaginal lips. The labia minora are a lot like the innermost petals of a flower – folds of super soft skin that cover and protect your vagina. Every girl is different: Some girls' labia minora are tucked into their labia majora, while other girls may have labia minora that peek out and are more visible.

CLITORIS This pea-sized organ is located where your labia majora and vagina come together in front, just below your mons pubis. It is super sensitive to the touch and is hidden by a "hood" to keep it protected.

THAT'S IT!

Our walk through the garden of mi'lady parts is complete. What may have seemed like a total mystery before, should now be a little more clear. Instead of thinking it's all complicated and scary down there, think about gardens (vulva) and flowers (labia)!

Well, that pretty much wraps up our pelvic tour! What have you learned about your pelvic region that you may not have known before?

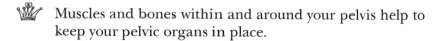 Muscles and bones within and around your pelvis help to keep your pelvic organs in place.

👑 The pelvis holds a major part of your digestive tract and houses all of the organs that help you eliminate waste as the food you eat travels from one end of you to the other.

👑 Your reproductive power centers on an incredible system of protective pouches, passageways, and caverns which support your monthly periods, and in pregnancy.

👑 Finally, and so important! The external part of your pelvic region – what you refer to as your private parts - is truly beautiful, delicate, special, and yours to protect and take good care of.

As you continue to read about your pelvic region, you now have the tools you need to visualize the pelvic parts you have just learned about. Can you "see" or "feel" any difference knowing what you now know? Is your pelvic region coming into focus?

CHAPTER THREE:
Do We Have to Go There?

NOBODY TALKS ABOUT POOPING and peeing, and yet every person on the planet, does it every single day. Going to the bathroom is part of being alive, just like eating and sleeping. It's kind of amazing we don't talk about it after we are two or three years old - except in whispers! Now that you know your pelvic region has three openings – the urethra, vagina, and anus - we need to talk about your daily duties in the bathroom. (Oh, yes we do!)

Good Bathroom Behaviors

You may think potty training is long over, but we're going to revisit it because it's BIG. In fact, this is where pelvic health and wellness starts.

WHEN YOU WERE A NEWBORN

your doctor asked your parents "is Baby (you) pooping and peeing?" You don't believe it? For the first few weeks of your life they had to keep a diary of how many times a day you went no. 1 or no. 2. She asked because it was one way of knowing your insides were working ok and that you were thriving.

WHEN YOU BEGAN TO TODDLE

around the house, it was time for potty training. As little kids we are taught to try to get to the toilet on time before having an accident. After that huge accomplishment, we learn to have good habits, like hand washing. Or not!

NO WORRIES

Many grown-ups don't know about the behaviors we're going to teach you here.

Pee and Me

We have two scenarios for you:

SCENE 1

You have just arrived at the movies to see the summer blockbuster, which hasn't started yet. You decide to pee - you know, just in case - because you don't want to miss any part of the movie. You enter the bathroom and thankfully everything looks clean. You decide not to sit on the seat so you hover like a bumblebee over the toilet instead. You pee. You wipe from the back to the front, and you clean up any dribble because you were taught to be a sweetie and wipe the seatie. You flush the toilet using your foot, and you wash your hands.

SCENE 2

After the movie you are out for pizza, and you truly have to pee.

You find the cute and pretty bathroom - a rare thing for a pizza place - but it's kind of dirty. You put some toilet paper on the seat, sit all the way down and go, wipe front to back, flush the toilet, and wash your hands.

Now, which of the two scenes do you think would be the best for you and your pelvis? We bet you've never even thought about your pelvis in the bathroom!

If you chose Number Two, you would be correct. (Ahem. Sorry for the poopy pun.)

Here's why Scene 2 was best:

Mind over Bladder

Way back when, just after your life in diapers, you were probably taught to go "JUST IN CASE." The grown-up in your life wanted you be comfortable - to take you out and about and play with you, without worrying about all the undressing and clean-up. To be fair, it's how we are all taught in the beginning.

THE NOT-SO-GOOD NEWS is that continuing to go when you don't really have a full bladder - just in case - is not healthy for you over time. If you happen to be one of those just-in-casers, you might start to feel like you always have to go, right now. URGENCY (the "gotta go right now") and FREQUENCY (the "always have to go") make millions of women spend more time in the bathroom instead of enjoying life.

JUST-IN-CASE PEEING (JIC-PEEING) creates on-going chatter between your bladder and your brain. Your bladder sends a signal to your brain telling it that you need to go. So you go, and that's ok, but when you JIC pee your bladder sends the message to your brain too often, and your smart brain starts to pick up on the message that it's good to go a lot.

BY GOING TO THE BATHROOM

before your bladder is full, your brain basically tricks it into feeling like it needs to empty right away, even though it might have lots of space left.

LET'S LISTEN IN

Speaking of space in your bladder, please don't be fooled into thinking yours is just dainty and little. If you feel you need to tinkle more than your friends do, you may need to pay attention to JIC-peeing.

Do you know anyone who's always looking for a bathroom? Your mom or aunt or grandma?

THIS COULD BE YOU SOMEDAY, SISTER!

If you can learn to "tune in" now to your body's signals and train your bladder to fill completely, you will be well on your way to kicking urgency and frequency.

Umm...

JUST IN CASE...

we're going to teach you this exercise to help you break the JIC habit and get you back on track.

Mind over Bladder Exercise

1 The next time you come home from some outing, say, skateboarding with your pals, and you feel like you have to pee, recognize the urge, but try not to act on it. Do something other than head straight to the loo. (British people say loo. So cute, don't you think?)

2 Instead, take a few deep breaths and relax. Brush your hair, help out in the kitchen, text a friend, something about JIC peeing (just kidding), whatever. Then, when you feel your bladder is truly full, go ahead and go. Doing this one simple thing for just a few weeks can really make a difference – at home.

3 The next step is to take Mind over Bladder into the world; for instance, back at the movies. Try not to pee right before the movie, and try to hold it all the way through. If you really need to pee in the middle of the movie, by all means, go. We wouldn't want you to have an accident. By the way, this doesn't work so well if you're downing 64-ounce sodas.

Mind over Bladder helps to reset the signals sent back and forth between your brain and your bladder.

On the flipside . . .

DON'T BE A CAMEL and hold it all in for 5 to 6 hours, or longer. Holding your pee for too long is also not a healthy habit and can cause a bladder infection. We talk about these later in the chapter.

TO PUT IT ALL INTO PERSPECTIVE a girl your age should be peeing every 3 to 4 hours while awake. That means about 4 times per day. During the night, you want to make it all the way through or get up only once.

How are your math skills? Can you figure out how many times you might pee in a year?

WHAT'S LBL?

LBL stands for "light bladder leakage" or as we like to say, "little bitty leaks." It's that experience you may have had, when you lose a little bit of urine and you didn't mean to – like if you've ever giggle peed! Any time you pee because you cough or laugh or sneeze or even while doing some sports – these are all LBL moments. If you *have* experienced an LBL moment, the first thing to know is that you are not alone – a lot of girls and women have LBL for one or more reasons. On the other hand, if LBLs have become a normal thing for you, please tell someone – your parent, caretaker, doctor – so you can get to a professional who can help you figure out what to do about it. Very often the "doing" is super simple – changing what you are eating or drinking, doing special exercises. We don't want to see you just "cope" or stop doing the things you love to do because you are afraid you might leak!

If at the beginning of this chapter you chose Scene 1 at the movies, you chose to JIC pee. You have now learned, NO MORE JIC-PEEING. In Scene 2 at the pizza parlor, there were other important bathroom behaviors you should know. Let's go over them . . .

Assume the Peeing Position

First . . .

PLEASE BE SEATED
It's better to sit all the way down. Don't hover like a bumble bee.

HERE'S WHY
When you do the bumble bee over the pot, your muscles tighten, and your bladder can't eliminate all your pee. And, that sends you back to the bathroom too soon, with a partly filled bladder, and there you are, needing to practice Mind over Bladder again. You may also spray, and that's not much fun for the next girl on the go!

If a toilet seat appears to be less than perfect, place toilet paper over it, and **"BUILD A NEST."** Sitting all the way down to pee **FREAKS** out so many girls and grown-ups! **IT'S OK TO SIT**! You will get over this fear once you realize how much *better* it is for you to sit. Your mom and her mom were probably taught to stand or hover over a public potty so they didn't pick up germs. Well, guess what? There are probably more germs on your cell phone than on a toilet seat.

Nest-building with TP, if the seat doesn't meet your satisfaction, is totally fine. You could also use those protective seat covers you sometimes see hanging above the toilets in public restrooms. In the back of this book, we include names of places where you can order or pick up your very own to carry in your backpack or purse.

Second . . .

THE FORCE IS NOT WITH YOU

Pushing or forcing strains and stretches out your **PELVIC FLOOR MUSCLES (PFM)**. These muscles are like a hammock – or a little like leggings. When you sit in them for a long time, you can stretch those cute leggings out. You know how in the rear they can kind of lose their shape and look baggy? You don't want baggy leggings, and you don't want baggy **PFM**. So not cute.

Pelvic floor muscles are a very important part of your anatomy—your bod:

IF IT'S HARD TO REMEMBER what PFM stands for, (see heading above), think of them as your PRETTY FABULOUS MUSCLES. That should help you remember them! We'll be showing you how to keep these muscles healthy and strong a little later.

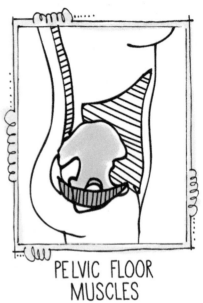

PELVIC FLOOR
MUSCLES

MEANWHILE BACK IN THE BATHROOM

Relaaaax . . . We point this out because it's the total opposite of forcing. Sit with your legs open, your feet flat on the floor, lean forward with your elbows on your knees, and don't rush. This will allow your bladder and urethra to be in the perfect position to get rid of all the urine stored there.

No matter what, take...your... time, because you have now learned that if you don't COMPLETELY EMPTY YOUR BLADDER, one day you will find yourself running to the bathroom to tinkle more than you text.

relaaax

HERE'S A LITTLE TRICK you can perform right now. Try this move we call, "Rock n' Roll":

Once you have urinated, take a second or two to rock your pelvis front to back and side to side. You do this by gently rocking your tail bone. If there's any more urine, it will trickle out on its own before you wipe and get on with your day.

PLASTIC BAG EXPERIMENT

To help you visualize what happens in your bladder when you Rock n' Roll: Take a small plastic zip top bag and pour in about a cup of water. Zip it up. This is your bladder full of pee. Place the bag in the palm of your hand, letting water pool and the bag fall through your fingers a bit. The water inside will settle into the gaps created by your fingers. If you move your hand around, you will see the water flow from your fingers into the main pool. Now, empty the bag and crumple it up. Like the baggy, your bladder when empty has creases and crevices where some extra urine can hang out. When you rock and roll, it tends to empty all the way.

Third. . . (We're in the bathroom again!)

TRY NOT TO GO THE WRONG WAY DOWN A ONE-WAY STREET

What does that mean!? It means WIPE FROM FRONT TO BACK in order to avoid infections caused by spreading bacteria from your rectum into your vagina and urethra. Yes, we're talking about wiping.

A common infection caused by wiping the other way, back to front, is called a URINARY TRACT INFECTION (UTI), which can be very, shall we say, ouchy. It's not the only way you can get a UTI, but it's a very common way.

FRONT — ONE WAY — BACK

WHAT'S A UTI?

A bladder infection is one type of UTI. Vaginitis is another type. These infections are so common most girls get one or the other at some point in their life. More annoying than anything else, vaginitis may be really itchy, while a bladder infection may feel like you have to pee –ALL THE TIME. Sometimes there may be a burning feeling while you pee - afterward too. And, occasionally an unusual odor will let you know something's going on. If a bladder infection travels up your urinary tract it can develop into another type of UTI called a kidney infection which is a bit more serious. More about UTIs in Chapter 9.

ROYAL WORDS OF WISDOM

A Bladder Myth

"I am the only girl who has ever giggle peed."

Not true! Up to 70% of all women will experience some type of bladder-related accident. Many women won't talk to their doctors about this because it's too embarrassing for them. As you're learning, it's okay to talk about these things because they are no longer taboo. Not only that, many bladder problems are preventable through good bathroom behaviors, exercise, and nutrition.

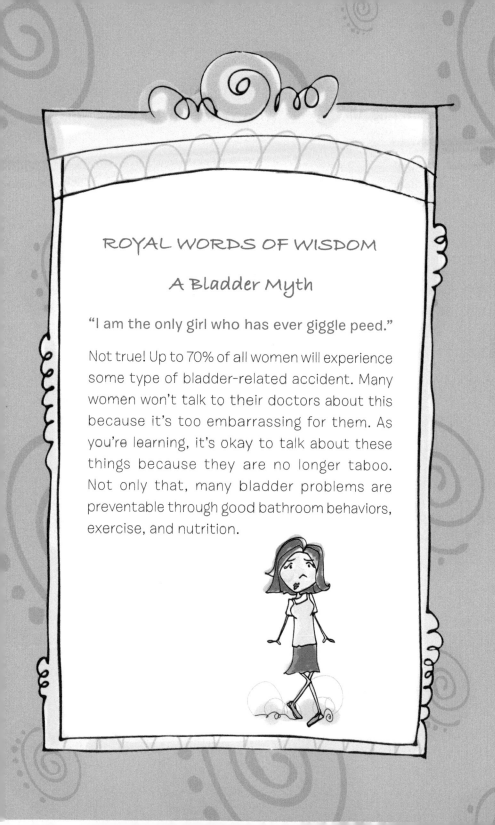

If you were never taught these Pee and Me Pointers, you are not alone!

The most important bathroom behaviors to remember are:

NOT SITTING ALL THE WAY DOWN

on the toilet puts stress and strain on your pretty fabulous muscles (PFM), weakening them over time.

FORCING PEE OUT

in a hurry does the same thing.

JIC-PEEING

just makes you have to pee more.

NOT EMPTYING YOUR BLADDER

all the way can lead to JIC-peeing and infection in some cases.

WIPING FROM BACK TO FRONT

can cause bacteria to travel into the urethra and cause an infection.

How can you remember the steps to good bathroom behaviors? Take the . . .

Potty Pledge®

✽ I will wipe Front to Back.

✽ I will sit all the way down on the potty
(even if that means building a nest)

✽ I will practice the "Rock and Roll."

✽ I will stop "Just-in-Case" peeing.

✽ I will drink water.

✽ I will treasure, honor and love my pelvis and most of all, love Myself.

CHAPTER FOUR:
Constipation Consternation

HAS THIS EVER HAPPENED to you? You are away at summer camp, the first week goes by, you're having so much fun and then you realize - you haven't pooped! You became (drum roll, please) CONSTIPATED!

TWO WORDS

CONSTIPATION (kon-stuh-PAY-shun): A condition in which a person - or animal - has difficulty eliminating solid waste, also known as fecal matter, stool or poop. A state in which the usual flow of something is blocked or stuck.

CONSTERNATION (kon-ster-NAY-shun): Shocked dismay: a feeling of alarm, confusion, or feeling bummed out, often caused by something unexpected – like not being able to poop!

Put them together and what do you get? Poop math!

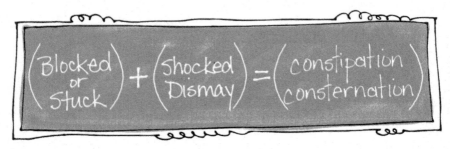

$$\left(\begin{array}{c}\text{Blocked}\\\text{or}\\\text{Stuck}\end{array}\right) + \left(\begin{array}{c}\text{Shocked}\\\text{Dismay}\end{array}\right) = \left(\begin{array}{c}\text{constipation}\\\text{consternation}\end{array}\right)$$

Remember how we talked about "taboo" in Chapter One? Going poop is a great example of a taboo topic.

PEOPLE POOP, ELEPHANTS POOP,

mice poop, super heroes poop, even princesses and queens poop. As natural as it is, pooping isn't easy for everyone. Did you know that some unfortunate people can't poop for days or even weeks? And, many people are afraid to talk about it, because it is not considered "socially acceptable."

That's Rough!

CAN YOU IMAGINE your teacher giving you and your class a lesson on pooping? With your BFFs and latest crush sitting so close? OMG.

Well, as you can see, we love talking about taboo "body" topics. This book recognizes good health has priority over what might seem awkward or uncomfortable to talk about.

If you are one of the lucky ones who have no problems pooping, snaps for you! If you are one of the many girls who get constipated, we have some helpful tips.

You may be wondering, "What in the world does this can't-poop talk have to do with my pelvis?"

WHEN YOUR PFM

are in good shape, they help you stay in control of both urination and bowel movements. If your muscles became weak, you would experience pee and poo when you least expected it, and before you could get to the bathroom.

THE LOSS OF CONTROL

is called **INCONTINENCE (in-CON-tin-ence)**. And, while there are many ways to become **INCONTINENT**, pushing hard and straining when you poo or when you can't poo, can cause your muscles to stretch like a worn out hammock or those leggings we talked about in Pee and Me.

Having an understanding of constipation and your PFM now will go a long way toward helping you avoid incontinence, the pee kind or the poo kind later in life.

So, what's one good way to keep those Pretty Fabulous Muscles nice and strong? Do your best to avoid constipation, and you won't have to strain and push.

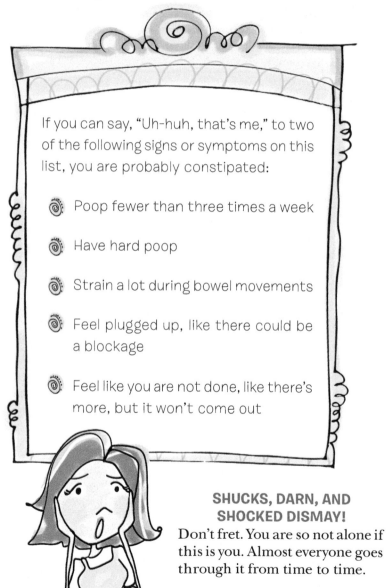

If you can say, "Uh-huh, that's me," to two of the following signs or symptoms on this list, you are probably constipated:

- Poop fewer than three times a week

- Have hard poop

- Strain a lot during bowel movements

- Feel plugged up, like there could be a blockage

- Feel like you are not done, like there's more, but it won't come out

SHUCKS, DARN, AND SHOCKED DISMAY!
Don't fret. You are so not alone if this is you. Almost everyone goes through it from time to time.

We'll need to look at the causes of constipation to understand how to not go there.

A LACK OF HYDRATION

is the biggest cause of constipation. Drinking enough water each day is an easy first place to start. You can actually see if you are drinking enough water by looking at the hydration chart in the back of the book. If your pee is a nice pale yellow, then it's likely you are well-hydrated (meaning you and your cells aren't thirsty), and you should have fewer problems pooping.

A LACK OF EXERCISE

and movement is another reason people get constipated. Think about how much physical activity you do each day. If you are into sports, you're probably just fine. If not, get moving!

JUMP ON A TRAMPOLINE!

Or up and down on the floor. Ride a bike. Dare we say it? Play outside, run around, get your sweat on. Be a kid—that means you, too, 14-year-olds.

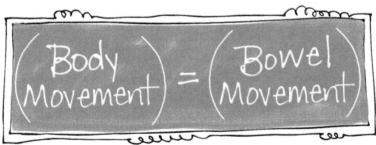

$$\left(\begin{array}{c}Body\\Movement\end{array}\right) = \left(\begin{array}{c}Bowel\\Movement\end{array}\right)$$

Stretch it out!

GENTLE STRETCHING CAN HELP
RELIEVE YOUR CONSTIPATION

and yoga helps to calm your consternation! Many yoga stretches are called poses, and they help people with everything from calming stress and anxiety to pooping! These gentle stretches and poses will help move things along. Remember: Never overstretch or strain. Think gentle.

Guess what? Not pooping can stress you out which makes it even harder to poop!

SEATED SPINAL TWIST

Sounds like contortion, but it's not! This little stretch will help wake things up inside.

1. Take a seat on the floor with both legs stretched out in front of you. Make yourself a little taller by lifting your body from your hips.

2. Cross your left leg over your right knee so you can place your left foot on the floor.

3. Place your right hand on your left knee, and your left hand behind your left knee, on the floor.

4. Gently twist up and to the left side, no further than your left knee. Really focus on the lower part of your spine.

5. Slowly come back to center.

6. Repeat, switching your legs and stretching to the other side.

FREE WIND

"Passing wind" is a charming way to say "passing gas," which is much better than saying, "Dude, I just farted." Often when you are constipated, your belly will feel full and bloated because gas gets trapped inside as well. This lovely sounding pose is easy and provides great relief.

1 Lie down on the floor, on your back.

2 Bend one leg from the knee and bring it up to your chest.

3 Hold your bent leg, all cozied up to your body, with both of your hands. Relax. Breathe.

4 Stay in this posture for a little while.

5 Repeat this pose with your other leg.

HAPPY BABY

One of our favorites, this pose makes us happy not only because of its name, but also because it's fun to do, and it works so well!

1 Lie down on the floor, on your back.

2 Bend both knees into your chest, toward your chin.

3 Open your knees, bringing them towards your armpits.

4 You can raise your head, but lower it again if it strains your neck.

5 Keeping your knees snug to your body, raise your feet to the ceiling and flex them (the opposite of pointing them).

6 Now reach up with your hands and grab the outer edges of your feet just like a baby.

7 Breathe. Hold this pose for a few minutes.

8 Giggle like a baby if you're in the mood.

Bigger Isn't Better

TO AVOID THE STRAIN AND PAIN
of the Big C, **SENSE** and **RESPOND**. Learn to sense, understand, and respond to your body's signals. Listen to your bowels: "Hello! Anyone out there? Let me out, let me out!"

IF YOU FEEL THE NEED TO POOP
and you ignore it, your poop can get bigger and harder to pass. Literally hard. Ow. Not good for you! Do try to respond right away. Just sayin'.

A word on excess pushing: Don't.

Two important points because we want you to feel more than comfortable where ever you are:

WE KNOW YOU HAVE ISSUES at school and other places, because we've been there, too. Lots of kids have school rules that make it hard to leave the classroom or take the time necessary to effectively poop. Just do the best you can when you are away from home.

WE ALSO KNOW that public restrooms can be tricky. Believe it or not, many grown-ups are uncomfortable pooping in public restrooms, too. The reasons? Because as a population, we're kind of shy! (Awww.) We are also embarrassed by our own – you know – smells? Or sounds? But relax, put yourself in your own private bubble, and go about your business.

PLEASE REMEMBER EVERYBODY poops! If you can get over this one big thing, you will be a healthier you.

THE SCOOP ON POOP
Here's a little tidbit.
Rabbit pellet poop
isn't a good thing.
To be specific,
you are looking
for toothpaste
consistency. Check
out the Bristol
Stool Chart in the
back pages of BYB
for a closer look!.

Hi, Fiber!

The very best thing you can do for constipation is . . .

EAT WELL

By well we mean quality, not quantity. "Eating healthy" is something you will hear – and hopefully do - for the rest of your life, but what does that really mean?

WE ASK YOU

Would you rather be processed and sludgy or fresh and perky?

WHO DOESN'T WANT A DOUGHNUT

or a handful of cheese puffs from time to time? We do! These foods satisfy sweet or salty cravings every once in a while (grown-ups call it "in moderation"), but caving to those cravings every day, over months and months and years and years does nothing for your bowels except clog them up.

IT MEANS YOU FOCUS ON

nourishing your body with the food you eat, so it runs well, not getting bogged down with chemicals and sticky, sugary stuff. There is a lot of truth to the idea you have probably heard before: "You are what you eat."

WHEN IT COMES TO CONSTIPATION

the best nourishment for your beautiful bod is fiber and water. Fiber is *Primo, numero uno.* In other words, *muy importante!*

FIBER IS THIS:

the parts of fruits and vegetables which cannot be digested in your belly. These itsy bitsy particles don't dissolve into your cells like other foods. Fiber's job is to help move the food you eat through your digestive tract. Think of it as a bulldozer.

No! A bowel-dozer!

Eating high-fiber foods such as beans, oats, whole grains, nuts, seeds, and raw fruits and vegetables will help keep the path to elimination clear.

NOW, HERE'S SOME COOL POOP MATH:

The amount of fiber you should try to eat every day is based on the number 10 and your age. For instance, if you happen to be 12 years old:

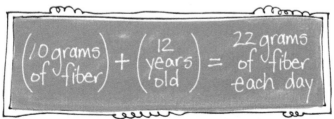

$$\begin{pmatrix} 10 \text{ grams} \\ \text{of fiber} \end{pmatrix} + \begin{pmatrix} 12 \\ \text{years} \\ \text{old} \end{pmatrix} = \begin{matrix} 22 \text{ grams} \\ \text{of fiber} \\ \text{each day} \end{matrix}$$

(This equation is not the same for adults.)

What would 22 grams of fiber look like?

A TRUCKLOAD OF BRAN CEREAL?

Thank food-goodness, no!

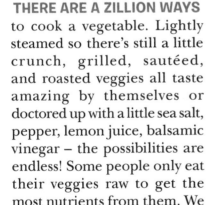

HERE'S AN EASY WAY TO THINK ABOUT IT

Girls ages 9 to 13 should eat at least 2 cups of vegetables per day, 1-½ cups of fruits per day, and a ½ cup of grains or legumes. Don't stop there! More is even better.

THERE ARE A ZILLION WAYS

to cook a vegetable. Lightly steamed so there's still a little crunch, grilled, sautéed, and roasted veggies all taste amazing by themselves or doctored up with a little sea salt, pepper, lemon juice, balsamic vinegar – the possibilities are endless! Some people only eat their veggies raw to get the most nutrients from them. We just want you to eat them!

Fruit is really easy. Pick it up, wash it off, eat it. Voila!

FIBER FINDS

Look for fruits and veggies from our Fiber Finds list at the back of the book. You may already have these items at home. If not, try something new – you may find a new favorite!

YOU COULD EAT THE FRUITS AND VEGETABLES FIRST

If you experience constipation consternation frequently, you may want to try this interesting way of eating whenever and wherever you meet up with food.

The reason this works for some: You fill up first on nutritious, good-for-you fruits and veggies which have all kinds of fiber, leaving a little less room for seconds on the triple fudge, quadruple cream brownies for dessert.

Some people just do better when they keep certain foods a little bit separated. Eating fruits and veggies first can help prevent a traffic pile-up in your digestive tract and bowels, giving your poop a smoother ride on its way out of town.

ONE YUMMY WAY TO GET SOME FIBER

in your diet and help keep you super regular, is to make HIGH-FIBER JAM. You might say "ew" to the ingredients, but it's really good! Share it with your family if you hear them complain about not being able to go.

For "success" in the morning, eat 1 TBS. of jam with a big glass of water every night with dinner or as dessert. If you don't notice an improvement within a couple of days, increase your portion to 2 TBS. every evening. For most people this is enough. Remember, always have a glass of water with the jam.

High Fiber Jam should be pretty thick and gooey. Keep it refrigerated in a covered container for up to a week.

1 cup applesauce
+
1 cup bran
+
½ cup prune juice (natural, no sugar)
High = Fiber Jam

What's Strange about Change

A big consternation creator is CHANGE. And, guess what? Things change all the time! Good changes, not-so-good changes, it doesn't matter. Whether travel, a move to a new place, a new school, or a new routine, all of these events can "change up" our systems and cause constipation. Our bowels can be pretty high maintenance! They need to be treated well.

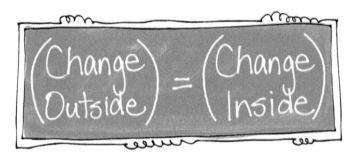

$$\left(\begin{array}{c}\text{Change} \\ \text{Outside}\end{array}\right) = \left(\begin{array}{c}\text{Change} \\ \text{Inside}\end{array}\right)$$

When change happens, it's time for water, for movement, and for fiber. Drink a tall glass of water, stretch a little, jump around, eat something fresh, and go in peace.

THE SUGGESTED TO-DOO LIST

DO: Get a stool for your stool! Sitting all the way down on the toilet seat while having your feet propped up, creates an angle which makes it easier for poo to make a clean get-away, and can really help relax your Pretty Fabulous Muscles.

DO: Relax. Straining and pushing can stretch your PFM.

DO: Belly breaths! It can be helpful to take slow, deep belly breaths. Open your mouth wide. Now breathe through your mouth as if you were trying to fill your belly with air. Blow the air back out slowly, too. Do this 3 to 5 times.

DO: Be a monkey! Raise your arms over your head. Let your hands relax. You can twist your hands back and forth for fun (hopefully no one walks in on you). Do this for a few minutes and see what happens.

DO: Read a book! Or listen to music or sing a song. Do something to distract you from what you are ultimately doing – pooing.

Next stop?
The great Pyramid!

CHAPTER FIVE:
Is the Pelvic Pyramid in Egypt?

 How does a dancer or ice skater spin gracefully without falling over?

 How does a volleyball player serve the ball with killer strength?

 Why do some kids look so confident when standing in front of the class?

EVERYTHING YOU HAVE LEARNED in this book so far is about pelvic *health*. Well, this chapter is about pelvic *strength* – which can lead to great *pelvic wellness* throughout your life.

Walk Like an Egyptian

IF YOU STOP TO CONSIDER
how strong or fit you are, you may think about your heart, arms, legs, stomach, and maybe your back muscles.

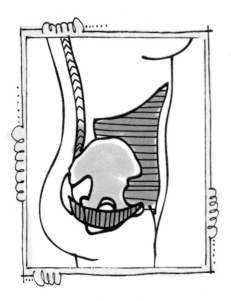

THE ALL TIME *BEST* MUSCLES to know about, below your belt, are your **PELVIC PYRAMID MUSCLES**. Together, they keep your pelvis and spine straight and strong; they support your organs like your bladder and uterus, and give you amazing strength and power all over.

SO NO!
The Pelvic Pyramid may not be in Egypt, but there are millions of Pelvic Pyramids *in* Egypt . . . walking around. Get it?

HAVE YOU EVER SEEN AN IMAGE OF KING TUT?

Frequently in ancient Egyptian hieroglyphs, pharaohs are shown sitting up straight, shoulders back, and chin centered, level with the floor. It has been guessed by some, that Egyptians believed sitting and standing with good posture would bring them special powers. When you think of "powers" you may think of super heroes; however, the Egyptians had something different in mind. It's possible they believed certain body positions "aligned" with the universe, and would provide healing. Good posture may have been thought to improve and control physical and mental health.

Standing Strong

You don't know it, but you use your Pelvic Pyramid muscles every day when you move around and do the things you love.

Your Pelvic Pyramid is there in the middle of all that activity – supporting your weight; supporting the fast movements of your arms and legs; supporting more controlled movements like those used in balancing; even supporting deep breaths when you swim or sing.

Knowing just a little bit about the muscles in your pelvic region will help you strengthen your foundation, which can help you rock whatever you do – on the soccer field, the basketball and volleyball courts, in gymnastics, or even standing in the front of your class, speaking with a strong voice and displaying all kinds of confidence.

Whatever your favorite sport or activity may be, that Pelvic Pyramid below your belt gives you your very own special Egyptian power.

Welcome to the Pyramid

THE PELVIC PYRAMID IS MADE UP OF
THREE DIFFERENT MUSCLE GROUPS

You can't see these muscles like you can see the muscles of your arms and legs. They are deep within you, and they surround your pelvis. Once you learn how to use them, you will really feel the difference!

On the Front Line

THE FIRST MUSCLE OF
THE PELVIC PYRAMID
is called your **TRANSVERSE ABDOMINAL (TVA)**. At the front of your Pyramid, the TVA wraps around your torso.

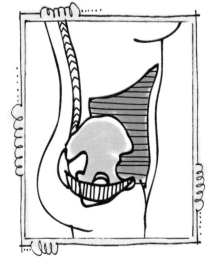

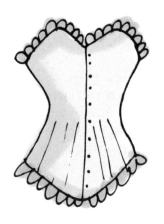

Ladies used to wear corsets every day to make their waists and tummies appear smaller and smoother. As if! Try slouching in one of those! Ouch! Today, we know that we can use our TVA, our built-in corset, to hold our shape, stabilize us, and give us super strength.

Hey! You in the Back!

THE SECOND MUSCLE OF THE PELVIC PYRAMID

Is called the **MULTIFIDUS**. Let's just call it your **MIGHTY MUSCLE (MM)**. It looks a little like a Christmas tree and runs right up your spine, helping to keep your back straight and strong. Your MM keeps your spine from collapsing and squishing all those important pelvic organs you learned about in Chapter Two.

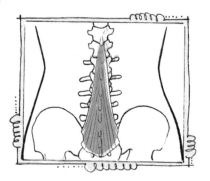

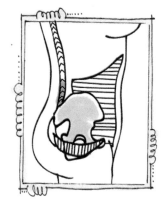

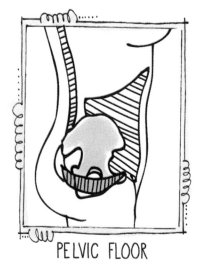

PELVIC FLOOR

PFMs Take the Floor

YOU KNOW THE THIRD GROUP ALREADY

the **PELVIC FLOOR MUSCLES** a.k.a. **PRETTY FABULOUS MUSCLES**. These are your BFFs. They protect you from LBL; they help keep your spine and pelvis in alignment; they are the base of the Pyramid.

A Different Approach

Your athletic coaches may have taught you and your friends that to be physically fit, you need to **WORK HARD**, push your bodies, and sweat and growl like monsters. OK, maybe not growl.

WHEN YOU START to engage your Pelvic Pyramid you will need to re-think the "she-man" method and be a little kinder and gentler to this part of your body. Not only that, you'll learn that the moves in this chapter are more mental than physical. As they say, "Less is more." (Who are they anyway?)

BEFORE YOU POWER UP THE PELVIC PYRAMID you have to do these two things first: You need to find your **NEUTRAL SPINE** and learn how to **RIBCAGE BREATHE**.

Neutral Spine

YOU HAVE YOUR OWN UNIQUE WAY OF SITTING AND STANDING

No one is the same. To find the best way for your body to stand or sit, you need to know how to find your neutral spine.

BASICALLY, NEUTRAL SPINE IS PERFECT POSTURE

Does the grown-up in your life ever tell you to stand up straight? Don't slouch? Well, after you've read this, you'll know why that's important, and better yet, you'll be able to show this person how to do it better! Standing or sitting "in neutral spine" will help you with your balance and even your breathing. Most importantly, finding your neutral spine will make it easier to get to your Pelvic Pyramid.

NEUTRAL SPINE IS A GOOD POSITION

for standing or sitting most of the time. It energizes you before any kind of exercise or if you are getting sleepy in class (of course that would never happen to you).

THE BEST WAY TO FIND IT

is to lie on the floor, on your back. Slide your feet toward your bottom.

◎ Place your hands under the "small" of your back, the natural curve of your spine, with your palms face-down.

◎ Press your back against your hands. Then, arch your back gently away from your hands, just to feel the difference.

◎ To get to the neutral position, find the spot where you are not pushing too hard on your hands, and you are also not arching your back. This is your neutral spine.

◎ You can also stand against a wall to find your neutral spine (a lot easier than lying down in public).

Breathe from Your Ribcage

YOU MAY HAVE HEARD YOU SHOULD BELLY BREATHE before singing or doing anything strenuous. We even talk a little about belly breathing at the end of the "Constipation Consternation" chapter. But to do Pelvic Pyramid exercises, you actually don't want to breathe too deeply because you want everything in your pelvic area to be "vewwy, vewwy quiet" as Elmer Fudd used to say when he tried to catch Bugs Bunny.

TO RIBCAGE BREATHE place one hand over your belly button and the other on your ribcage. Inhale. You may find that both of your hands move a bit. To visualize what's happening, pretend your ribcage is an accordion when you breathe. Your ribs will expand and your belly will show little movement.

INHALE AGAIN

Imagine your ribcage expanding outward, front, back and sideways. Your belly may rise and fall again – that's normal. This is ribcage breathing, and you do it only when doing the exercises in our book.

If you find ribcage breathing too difficult, the most important thing to remember is just to breathe. As long as you don't hold your breath, you are doing great! Now that you have charged yourself up, it's time to power up. Quick word about a super hero first.

You know who Wonder Woman is, right? The warrior princess of the Amazon? As a totally awesome super hero complete with tiara, boots, and lasso, she's the perfect example of STRONG. That Pelvic Region below her belt is where she gets her strength, power, and stability.

Power up your Pelvic Pyramid

1. Have you hugged yourself lately?

Here's an eye-opening experiment:
You'll need a friend to do it with!

STAND FACING EACH OTHER

in neutral spine position, feet shoulder width apart. Totally relaxed, have your friend place her hands on the front of your shoulders. Now, ask her to give you a little push.

What happened?

**NEXT, GENTLY PULL YOUR BELLY
BUTTON TOWARD YOUR SPINE**

and think of the TVA muscle wrapping from your belly around to your back, giving you a gentle hug. Hold this TVA "hug" a few moments so you get familiar with how it feels.

TRY IT AGAIN

and this time before your friend pushes you, give yourself a TVA hug and hold it. Did you move? You didn't, did you?! You probably felt way more stable. This is your TVA muscle in action.

YOU CAN GIVE YOURSELF A TVA "HUG" ANYWHERE YOU ARE

It's such a small movement no one, not even you, will see it. You can get a hug in the lunch line, while you are sitting in class or while you're hanging out with friends. That warmth you might feel in your mid-section is you, powering up!

Gold medal, anyone? If you start all your activities with a lovin' TVA hug, when you kick a ball, you will kick stronger. When you are spinning or turning, you will spin faster, and while jumping, you will jump higher. Go on, give it a try! Remember to hug often to be stronger, more powerful and stable.

2. Confidence is only an inch away

EVERYONE IS BEAUTIFUL in her own unique way. That being said, models and celebrities in magazines are usually "photoshopped" in one way or another. The magazine's design team makes their teeth look straight and white, their skin flawless, and they even cut curves to make them look unnaturally thin, or they add curves in certain places making a person look like they have bigger boobs or poutier lips.

THE TRUTH IS looking at a magazine photo is not the same as looking at the real person. Most people know that beauty is a wonderful combination of many personality traits and **CONFIDENCE**. Beauty on the inside is the real deal.

IF YOU WOULD LIKE TO IMPROVE your overall appearance, believe it or not, posture (standing up straight) is the best way to get there. Getting into neutral spine, working your **MIGHTY MUSCLE**, and using your **TVA** to help improve your posture will instantly make you look and feel more confident.

YOUR MIGHTY MUSCLE IS EASY AND FUN TO EXERCISE
Grab a small book. Stand up straight, give yourself a TVA hug, then balance the book on your head. Try to stretch your spine an inch or two, from your hips. No standing on your toes! It's important that your head is level (which is why you have a book on your head). Once you get the feel of it, you won't need the book anymore.

ANOTHER WAY TO STRETCH THAT MM
is to grow an inch or two while seated. Anchor your rear end to the seat of your chair and stretch from your tail bone.

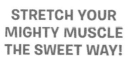

STRETCH YOUR MIGHTY MUSCLE THE SWEET WAY!
Imagine your spine is like a candy necklace. Give yourself that TVA hug before you begin, then "stretch" the candy necklace apart, making a space between your **VERTEBRAE (VUR-te-bray)**, the little bones that stack up to create your spine.

Hello, Mrs. President! Have you ever seen bad posture on a princess or the Queen of England or the First Lady? We didn't think so. They may not know it, but these ladies work their MM.

3. A quick hello to your PFMs...

BEFORE WE HAVE A PFM CHECK-IN we need to point out that even though we tend to think in **THREES** when it comes to pyramids, at this stage of your life we're only going to have you focus on **TWO** – your TVA and your MM.

WE TALKED A LOT about healthy pelvic floor muscles in Chapters Three and Four, but we don't actually want you to do PFM exercises until you are fully grown.

Just as an orchestra doesn't always play all the instruments at once, the same goes for the Pelvic Pyramid. Even though you only work two sides, the three sides are still working in concert (together).

TO HELP YOU UNDERSTAND THE LOCATION OF YOUR PFM imagine how it feels when you stop the flow of pee or when you squeeze your tush to keep a toot from escaping in class – these little movements put you in contact with your PFM.

TVA hugs and MM stretching power up the whole region of your pelvis. So, even if you don't exercise your PFM directly, they become royally energized anyway.

Anytime you want to work on your physical skills, like sports, dance and even better posture, all you have to do is picture your own Pelvic Pyramid, lifting you up, creating stability and strength for any kind of movement. You're charged and ready to go. Let's exercise!

CHAPTER SIX:
K.I.S.S. – Keep It Strong, Sister!

AS QUEEN OF YOUR PELVIC REGION you will want your kingdom to maintain its balance and to provide protection from invaders like weakness or illness. Your pelvis wants to support you! Doing the poses and exercises in this chapter will help you and your pelvis become great teammates. You do a little. Your pelvis does a little. A very nice friendship, indeed.

Speaking of teammates, yours will notice your improved strength and control in very short time.

DOING THESE SMALL EXERCISES BEFORE BED
or when you're watching a movie at home, or anytime you can fit them in, will bring big benefits to your body and help keep you connected to your powerful pelvis. Always breathe, listen to your body to know if you are pushing too hard, and move in comfort.

GET TO KNOW THEIR NAMES!

1. Flamingo
2. Clam
3. Controlled Banana Peel
4. Bicycle Chain
5. Mini Cobra
6. Hunting Dog
7. Planks: Porcupine and Stepladder
8. Cats and Cows

REMEMBER TO ENERGIZE YOUR PELVIC PYRAMID
before or during every pose and exercise. We'll tell you exactly when. Also, try to visualize or "see" your Pelvic Pyramid whenever you do these. It's kind of like "snapchatting" with your pelvis!

Flamingo

TO IMPROVE YOUR BALANCE AND STRENGTHEN YOUR ANKLES

1 Stand up straight with your arms stretched out to either side.

2 *Energize your Pelvic Pyramid... Now!*

3 Lift one leg slowly, bending it at the knee like a flamingo. Do your best to balance without putting your foot back down or resting it against your standing leg.

4 Now think about "pushing" the floor away with your standing foot. Don't raise your heel. Use your whole foot. This little bitty move is more of a "focus" – mental telepathy for your pelvis. It helps you engage your Pelvic Pyramid.

5 Hold your Flamingo for a count of 10–30 Mississippi's, then switch legs.

POINTER Don't let your ship sink, ahemm, your *hip* sink, and keep your MM nicely stretched.

HARDER OPTION When you feel it's too easy, close your eyes and swing your arms.

Clam

TO STRENGTHEN YOUR OUTER HIP MUSCLES

Weakness can lead to an unstable pelvis, meaning an unstable you! Especially when you're older.

1 On a soft surface, lie on your side with your hips "stacked" on top of each other. Your knees will be slightly in front of your hips.

2 *Time to energize your Pelvic Pyramid!* Breathe normally.

3 Imagining how a clam-shell opens and closes, keep your feet together while you lift your top knee. Don't force your knee higher than it can comfortably go.

4 Create your own resis-tance by thinking about pushing that top knee (top half of the shell) through the mud just like a clam would. Your Pelvic Pyramid will help keep you still. If you feel a little burning sensation in your butt muscles, you are doing it correctly!

5 Now, don't fall back on your rear end! Grab a TVA hug to stop the rest of your body from moving around. "Clam" twenty times at a pretty good pace, not as slow as syrup, not as fast as water. Raise your clamshell up for 1 Mississippi and down for 1 Mississippi.

6 Switch sides!

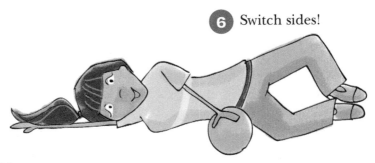

Controlled Banana Peel

TO HELP STRENGTHEN YOUR TVA

1 Lie on your back with your knees bent, feet on floor, in neutral spine.

2 *Energize your Pelvic Pyramid!*

Consider what this exercise would feel or look like if you did not energize your Pelvic Pyramid beforehand. Pretty sloppy, right?

3 Imagine you've got one heel on a banana peel. Slide it out, away from your body, until your leg is straight. Keep your pelvis very still by holding a TVA hug.

4 Slowly slide your heel back toward your body to the starting position, keeping your belly and pelvis still. Hold that hug!

5 Slide on the pretend banana peel 10 times with your left leg and 10 times with your right leg.

COMMON MISTAKES Taking your heel off the floor, arching your back, forgetting about your TVA hug, and shifting your pelvis around.

Bicycle Chain

TO IMPROVE YOUR SPINE'S FLEXIBILITY AND FEEL AWESOME

See if your grown-up can do this one. At the beginning it may be difficult, but with practice, anyone can do it. In this exercise you are going to pretend your spine is like a bicycle chain, moving one link at a time.

1 Lie on your back, knees bent, feet on the floor, shoulder width apart.

2 Find your neutral spine. Breathe normally. Inhale and *energize your Pelvic Pyramid!*

3 Tuck your tail bone, and squeeze your bottom. Exhale and slowly peel your pelvis one vertebra at a time, off the floor, just like the links of a bike chain.

4 Stop about half way up your spine, inhale at the top, then exhale and roll back down one vertebra at a time. Think clink, clink, clink.

5 Do this 4 times up and down total. Count 5 Mississippi's on the way up, and 5 on the way down.

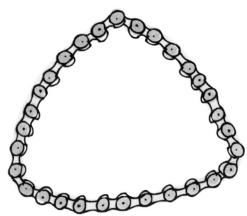

POINTER Try to keep your shoulders and neck very relaxed. If it feels like your shoulders are about to kiss your ears, relax, and lower them. Try to keep your tail bone tucked – also known as a **PELVIC TILT**.

This move can take some practice! At first you may feel like you can't separate your vertebrae, like they're moving in a chunk all at once. We can tell you, keep practicing! Before long you'll be able to feel them moving one by one.

COMMON MISTAKES Skipping vertebrae. Going too fast. You can now see that if you don't move these parts, they can get kind of frozen up – like an old rusty bicycle chain.

Mini Cobra

TO HELP STRENGTHEN YOUR BACK AND KEEP YOU FLEXIBLE
Imagine a cobra, raising its head and its body up, totally defying gravity. We're going to help you do that, too.

1 Lie face down, chin pointed to the floor. Place your hands under your shoulders, elbows bent, touching the floor. Keep them close to your body.

2 Keep your ankles close to each other and point your toes so the tops of your feet are touching the floor.

3 *Energize your TVA* by pulling your belly slightly off the floor, and relax your shoulder blades.

4 Inhale, then exhale, imagining the air being released from your back. Draw your shoulder blades down, and lengthen your spine.

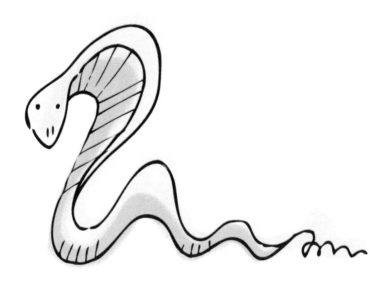

5 Lift your chest up, while stretching your spine out a few inches from the floor, keeping your arms in their position. Imagine cookies under your forearms. Try not to crush them! This is a very small move – you won't rise up very high.

6 Keep your eyes focused somewhere in front of you toward the floor.

7 Hold your Cobra pose in the "up" position for 5 Mississippi's while breathing steadily, rest for 3, and do it 2 more times.

COMMON MISTAKES Pressing up too far, having a lazy belly (lack of TVA engagement), or stretching your neck too far back.

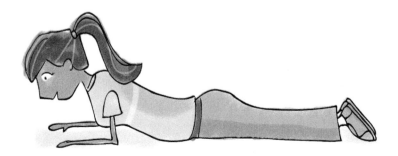

Planks: Porcupine

TO TONE AND STRENGTHEN YOUR WHOLE BOD-STOMACH, BACK, SHOULDERS, CHEST AND ARMS

Maybe you have seen someone "do" a plank, where your body looks like a picnic bench. Our planks are much easier and super-sneaky strengtheners. Take a look!

1 Get onto all fours, in other words, onto hands and knees.

2 *Energize your Pelvic Pyramid*, and ribcage breathe.

3 Now walk your hands out in front of you until it feels a little bit challenging. Your knees should remain on the floor.

4 Drop your forearms to the floor and relax your shoulders. Shift your body forward, just a little.

5 Grow an inch in your spine and get a TVA hug for strength and stability.

6 Keeping your back flat and strong (think plank), imagine a porcupine is about to walk right under your belly. What would you do if this really happened? You would pull in your belly and give yourself a TVA hug!

7 Hold for 5-10 Mississippi's, rest for 5, and do it 3 more times.

COMMON MISTAKES Walking your hands out too far. Shifting your weight too far forward. Lazy belly – no TVA hug.

and Stepladder

1 This time, start on your forearms and knees. Make sure your toes are tucked under your feet.

2 *Energize your Pelvic Pyramid,* and ribcage breathe.

3 Relax your shoulder blades and press your knees up into pike position so you look like a stepladder. Center your weight at your hips and press back slightly into your feet. You'll feel this stretch in your calf muscles and hamstrings (the muscles at the back of your thighs).

4 Stretch your MM, and give yourself a TVA hug for strength. Don't forget to breathe.

5 Hold this position 5-10 Mississippi's, rest for 5, and do it 3 more times.

COMMON MISTAKES Shifting your weight too far forward. Resting on your hands instead of your forearms. Lazy belly – no TVA hug.

Hunting Dog

TO HELP ENERGIZE THE PELVIC PYRAMID
ESPECIALLY YOUR MM

as well as your back and hip muscles, your upper back, and the muscles of your shoulders.

1 On hands and knees, with your neck in perfect alignment with your spine, *energize your Pelvic Pyramid*. Ribcage breathe.

2 Inhale and extend one leg behind you, keeping it level with the rest of your body (not too high and not too low).

3 While growing an inch in the spine try to lift the opposite arm straight out in front of you, don't lift higher than your outstretched leg.

4 Stretch the candy necklace necklace of your MM.

5 Hold this pose for 5 Mississippi's then switch legs. Do both sides 3 more times. Remember to breathe!

COMMON MISTAKES Arching your back, lack of TVA hug, head tilted upward, and lifting your arm or leg too high.

Cats and Cows

GREAT FOR THE END OF ANY WORKOUT

These two poses will keep you stretchy and flexible, and make all the other exercises you do nice and easy.

1 Begin on your hands and knees in neutral spine.

2 Inhale to prepare, now exhale while pulling your tailbone down and under as your chin drops toward your chest. Gently stretch out your spine, like a cat.

3 Inhale again and arch your back, raising your head and your tailbone to the sky. Let your belly sag so it's totally relaxed, like a cow.

4 Do this 3 or 4 times: cat-cow-cat-cow.

COMMON MISTAKE Not moving enough! Stretch it all out, but remember to keep it comfortable.

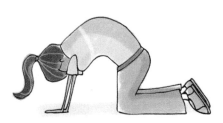 

You can build a strong foundation for your pelvic region if you remember to do these super moves throughout your life.

THE EASIEST WAY TO STAY HEALTHY

with all your parts moving as they should? Regular cardiovascular "cardio" exercise: running, jumping, skipping, hopping, skating, riding, walking, swimming, dancing.

Keep your blood pumping each day through that most wonderful of muscles, your heart, and you will be in great shape. No matter how you time it, you want to have rosy cheeks and slightly elevated breath – no need to pass out – just go have 30-60 minutes of physical fun every day, and practice the K.I.S.S. concept, your ticket to fabulous health. In the meantime, let's go meet a very special someone in your pelvic royal court.

CHAPTER SEVEN

Congratulations, Your Highness!

YOU MAY BE CLOSE TO GETTING YOUR PERIOD

for the first time or you might be a pro already. Whichever is true for you, in your mind do you just "get your period" each month? Or, do you think there's something more going on? The words period and menstruation hold different meanings for different girls.

What's In a Name?

THREE MORE NEW WORDS FOR YOU:

REPRODUCTIVE (ree-pro-DUC-tiv): The system within your pelvic region that creates and supports new life

PUBERTY (PYOO-ber-tee): The age when your reproductive organs become "activated," creating the start of periods, the growth of pubic hair, and many other fun changes in the body

CYCLE (CY-cul): Not something you ride – It's when an event or situation repeats itself in the exact same way over the same period of time

MENSTRUAL is an ancient English word dating back to the 13th century referring to "monthly," which also stems from "moon" because the moon circles the earth on a cycle lasting about 28 days, which is about a month.

CYCLE as we have pointed out, refers to something that is repeated in the same way over the same period of time, over and over. **PERIOD** refers to the "period" of time during your menstrual cycle when you see blood. (Are you having a light bulb moment yet?)

So, these words all mean the same thing – the process of shedding bits of endometrial lining and blood from your uterus, usually once per month, upon reaching puberty.

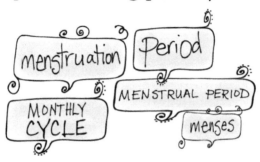

THE GIRL AND THE MOON

What do the moon and getting your period have in common? Because the moon affects our oceans' tides, making them ebb (go out) and flow (come in), it follows that the moon could also have an effect on our bodies, which are made mostly of water, too.

Throughout time, many people have believed that this magic "pull" of the moon also affects a woman's menstrual cycle! Though not all girls menstruate on a precise 28-day cycle, it is the most common stretch of time from period to period. Do you think the moon has anything to do with the timing of your menstrual cycle?

Take a Look Inside

Is it surprising to learn you were once inside your
grandmother's body? Your menstrual cycle is linked to
past and future generations of women in your family.

IMAGINE THE WOMAN

in this picture was your grandmother as a young lady, and the baby
was your mom. The dot is you as an egg, in your mom's ovaries!
Confusing, isn't it? That's how you could be inside both your mom
and your grandmother at the same time. And, that means, when
you were born, you also had a full supply of ova neatly tucked
inside your very own ovaries.

If you can see the connection you have to your mom and grandmom, and add all the generations before them, then the whole process of getting your period starts to mean so much more than just pads and tampons.

Could this be the reason women and girls have such a strong bond?

Don't get us wrong! Dads, uncles, and grandpas are all pretty awesome, too. In some cases they're the ones to go to for period support and are just as loving and caring. Be comforted in knowing you are not alone.

When Mother Nature Knocks

**PERIODS HAPPEN
ONCE A MONTH**
(actually every 24 to 36 days)
from the time you hit puberty
until you reach about the age
of 50. So, it's not forever.

WE KNOW, WE KNOW
the thought of bleeding every
single month may not have
been something you signed up
for, but how you think about
your period can affect you for
the rest of your life.

If you think of your
period NEGATIVELY,
you will most
likely really dread
each month.

IF YOU JUST LOOK AT THE NUMBERS
a period lasts about 5 days every month. There are 12 months
in a year (12 x 5 = 60). So, for 60 days each year you could be
super bugged.

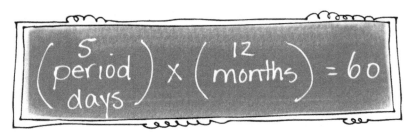

$$\left(\begin{array}{c}5 \\ \text{period} \\ \text{days}\end{array}\right) \times \left(\begin{array}{c}12 \\ \text{months}\end{array}\right) = 60$$

YOU HAVE YOUR PERIOD FOR ABOUT 40 YEARS
that's 60 x 40 - which is 2,400. UGH! To be bugged for two thousand, four hundred days of your life!? No, thank you!

WHY NOT BE THAT GIRL
who really understands her menstrual cycle and feels special and proud on those 2,400 days? You can breathe out now because that's what we're talkin' about!

If you think about it POSITIVELY, you'll sail smoothly along for all your reproductive years.

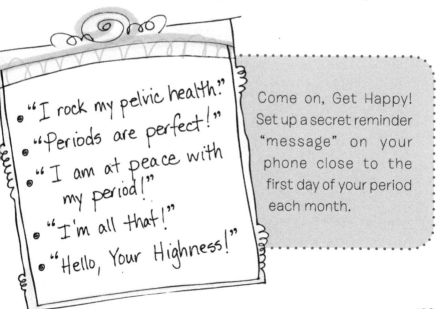

- "I rock my pelvic health."
- "Periods are perfect!"
- "I am at peace with my period!"
- "I'm all that!"
- "Hello, Your Highness!"

Come on, Get Happy! Set up a secret reminder "message" on your phone close to the first day of your period each month.

Tradition!

FAMILIES ALL OVER THE WORLD

celebrate when their daughters have their first period. Don't be shy! This is a proud and meaningful moment in your life. Get your ears pierced, have a manicure in a salon, buy a new belt as a secret nod to the new activity in your pelvic region!

FAMILY TRADITIONS ARE WONDERFUL

and can make you feel very connected to the generations before you. Creating your own tradition, if there isn't already one in place, can make future generations of girls in your family – your little sister, your daughter, and granddaughter – feel very special.

A New Tradition

We have talked about making connections to other women, to special caregivers, and to what's going on inside you each month. Get to know your mom, grandma, aunts, great aunts, and older sisters by asking them some questions about their own experiences.

EXPLAIN THAT YOU ARE READING

Below Your Belt and you were guided to ask three women you care about and trust, personal questions about their own menstruation. Don't be afraid to interview your female teachers and sitters, too, and feel free to talk to as many women as you like.

YOU'LL FIND A SCRIPT

in the back of this book if you want some help getting started. You can always ask your own original questions, too.

BE SURE TO THANK THE WOMEN

for sharing their personal stories and experiences in an effort to be helpful to you. And, consider creating a new tradition by sharing this activity with your own daughter one day, passing it on for her to interview the women in her life – undoubtedly one of them will be you!

EXTRA CREDIT Ask a man! If you are comfortable, and we hope you will be, ask a close family member – like a dad or a brother – how he feels about girls' periods. You may want to start with, "I'd like to ask you about something kind of personal. Do you have time?"

Wait, wait, there's more! More than the period. More than the blood.

Introductions

We girls spend quite a bit of time focusing on the visible part of getting our periods, the blood. Along the way, you may never have learned what happens in the days before you get your period.

To help describe the "before" part, we will tell you a fairy tale about the journey of a famous but little understood member of your pelvic royal court:

Queen of your Pelvic Region, meet Ovum, Princess of Ovulation.

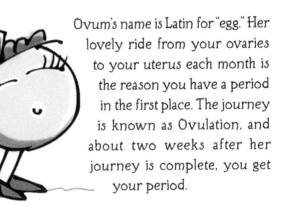

Ovum's name is Latin for "egg." Her lovely ride from your ovaries to your uterus each month is the reason you have a period in the first place. The journey is known as Ovulation, and about two weeks after her journey is complete, you get your period.

Quite a Schedule

Let's look at the Princess of Ovulation's monthly social calendar. You'll soon see how worthy she is and why she deserves to be treated like royalty.

Ovum starts her journey each month in her home, an ovary, where she and her millions of sisters, Ova, have been seated quietly since long before you were born.

As soon as you reach puberty — the age you are old enough for this incredible journey inside of you to begin — a few of the bravest of the Ova will wake up, wrap themselves up in a bubble called the corpus luteum (corpus loo-TEE-um) and quietly knock on the wall of either one of your two ovaries. One of these darlings is able to sneak her way out without you knowing.

Though you could feel a little twinge on either side of your pelvis as the Princess of Ovulation pushes her way outside of her protective palace, you usually won't feel a thing.

Ovum is then gently swept into the nearest Fallopian Tube by a "fringe" group called the FIMBRIAE (FIM-bree-eye).

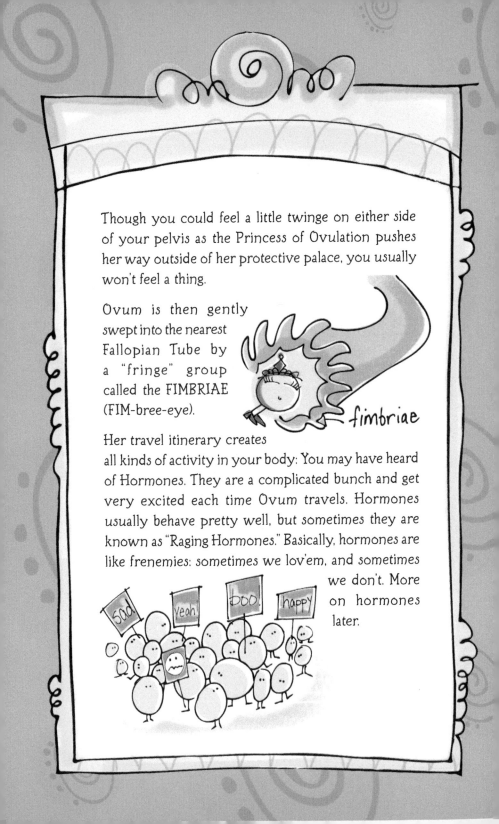

fimbriae

Her travel itinerary creates all kinds of activity in your body: You may have heard of Hormones. They are a complicated bunch and get very excited each time Ovum travels. Hormones usually behave pretty well, but sometimes they are known as "Raging Hormones." Basically, hormones are like frenemies: sometimes we lov'em, and sometimes we don't. More on hormones later.

sad   yeah!   boo.   happy

Sometimes you may see a little "spotting" in your underwear between one period and the next. This happens when levels of certain hormones shift around. It's totally normal, but not every girl experiences it.

During her journey, the Princess of Ovulation will travel from your Ovary, through its corresponding Fallopian Tube, and will finally come to rest in the comfort of a very cushy, warm place – your uterus.

(Meanwhile, Endometrium, the beautiful uterine lining who protects the Princess, has been preparing for her arrival.)

Here's where the awe-inspiring amazingness of Ovum becomes clear. She will hang out with Endometrium in your uterus either one of two ways:

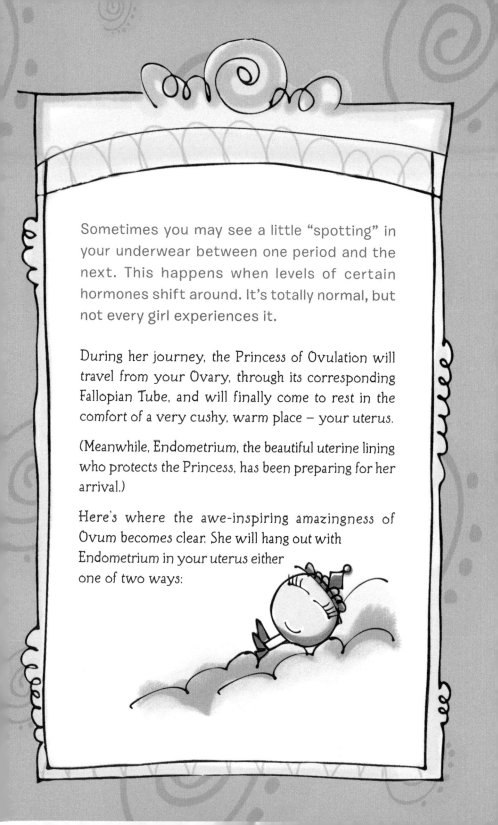

A By joining a sneaky suitor, let's just call him Sir Sperm, in a Fallopian Tube and settling in with him to create a fetus — the very early development of millions of cells which eventually become a baby human. For nine whole months this "new and improved" version of the Princess will make your uterus her home.

OR

B By the no less dramatic and more likely scenario of magically vanishing, being reabsorbed back into your body, about a week after arriving.

Following Option B, The Princess of Ovulation may have come to the end of her journey, but she doesn't go unnoticed.

Show Time!

Finally, the day or night comes. You get your period! For 3-7 days (everyone is different), bits and pieces of lining (our friend, Endometrium) are shed through your vagina, clearing out her old padding and creating a clean environment for one of the Ova-sisters to make her own journey next month.

The Moral of the Story

Your menstrual cycle involves ovulation and your period, also connection, tradition, a great attitude, and celebration!

Let's go learn some of the ins and outs of menstruation.

CHAPTER EIGHT

Practical Matters

HAVING A PERIOD IS JUST AS NORMAL

as peeing, pooping, sneezing, coughing, and laughing, but there's still a lot of mystery around how to take care of yourself. Just think, each month thousands and thousands of girls get their period for the very first time, and many of these darlings don't know what to do. Let's talk about the things you can do in your daily life as you cycle month to month.

CAN YOU IMAGINE never being taught about getting your period and thinking you are absolutely dying the first time you see blood? Despite living in the 21st century, it still happens to girls all over the world.

People can get a little squeamish around blood, but **PERIOD BLOOD** is different than **INJURY BLOOD**. When you have your period, you "bleed" from the same part of your body every month, not wherever you have a cut or scrape.

SOME WOMEN DON'T EVEN LIKE TO CALL IT BLEEDING because blood from an injury hints at something that needs to heal, while having a period is a natural part of every woman's life.

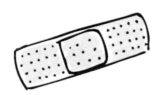

Having a period is part of a natural **CLEANSING PROCESS** with no injury in sight. The blood itself, as you learned in our ovulation fairy tale, contains endometrial lining from your uterus.

IN FACT HAVING A PERIOD IS A LITTLE BIT LIKE CLEANING YOUR HOME

Some rooms you clean, like your bedroom; and others are cleaned for you— possibly your classroom or kitchen. Well, on your body, you clean up some "rooms" every day like armpits and teeth, and some are naturally cleaned up for you every month – your uterus for instance.

DON'T WORRY

if the color of your menstrual blood is not what you expected. It can be pink or red, the deepest purpley-blue, even brown or black! The color will change during your period depending on how long it takes for endometrial lining to be released from your body.

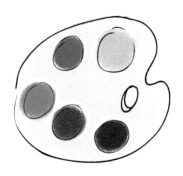

What do 4 tablespoons have to do with menstruation? That's about the amount of blood most girls and women shed each period.

I See London, I See France

WHAT'S THAT STUFF IN MY UNDERPANTS?!

The mysterious "stuff," usually white or yellowish in color, is produced by your cervix (look back to Chapter 2 or the Glossary for a reminder) and is called **CERVICAL FLUID**. Many girls have a hard time understanding and accepting that cervical fluid is completely normal and healthy. For those of you who are not crazy about the word "fluid," let's just call it **CERVICAL FUN (CF)**!

SOMETIMES GIRLS WILL HAVE CF

before the onset of their first period. It's common and indicates their body is getting ready to start menstruation.

HOW IT LOOKS

and what color it is, changes throughout your menstrual cycle each month. You'll notice, for instance, that right after your period you'll have close to none. Toward the middle of your cycle, you'll find it kind of sticky.

Don't feel weird about it – it shows you are healthy. And, it's completely normal.

Very Fitting – Pads and Tampons

CHOOSING WHAT TYPE OF PROTECTION
to use during your period can be challenging! How do you know which might work the best for you?

PADS ARE WORN ON
THE OUTSIDE
in your underwear. They come in many sizes and thicknesses to match the heaviness or lightness of your flow.

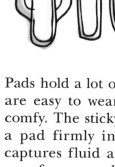

Pads hold a lot of fluid. They are easy to wear and pretty comfy. The sticky strip keeps a pad firmly in place as it captures fluid and whisks it away from your skin while you make your way through the day – or night.

Pads are a great choice when you are not quite ready to try a tampon.

TAMPONS ARE WORN ON THE INSIDE
You insert a tampon into your vagina, and it collects the flow of blood. They can be trickier to figure out, but by following the directions included in the box and a little practice, you'll do just fine.

137

Tampons are a great choice when you want to keep your focus on your activities while not worrying about a pad getting in the way.

NOT ALL AGREE

that tampons are safe because a potentially serious infection known as Toxic Shock Syndrome has been connected to wearing **synthetic** tampons and leaving them in for too long. We're happy to report that they are very safe when regularly changed, and opposed to what many people have learned, it is also safe to sleep with a tampon in, without having to get up in the middle of the night to change it. Just always remember to take it out upon waking up. Go with 100% cotton. It will say so clearly on the box.

LIKE CINDERELLA'S GLASS SLIPPER

you may find a pad or tampon is too wide or too narrow, too long or too short, too loose or too tight! Try them all—just like shoes.

ONCE YOU HAVE FIGURED OUT HOW THINGS FIT

we recommend having a few of each type at home: daytime and nighttime pads, tampons when you are ready for them, and panty liners, which are good for the beginning or end of your period and when you have more cervical fluid than usual.

What's a "menstrual cup"? It's a rubbery cup you place inside your vagina where it catches blood. It can stay right where it is up to 12 hours, before it is removed and rinsed out, making it possible to use again and again over many months. Cups are recommended for girls and women who are extremely comfortable with their bodies and those who are particularly interested in the environment.

ALWAYS FOLLOW "HOW TO" DIRECTIONS

on the box or bag of tampons or pads— including how often to change them, usually every 3-4 hours. In time, you'll even get to know the heaviness of your flow and how long you can go with a pad versus a tampon.

When you do change your pad or tampon, please make sure to wrap it up in either the wrapper it came in or in toilet paper, before you throw it away. The person who takes out the garbage will greatly appreciate it!

Make sure you do this at home, too. It's called common courtesy, and that is something queens from all regions know.

And, whatever you do, please don't flush it because it's really hard on the environment and the pipes. Plunger, please!

Follow Your Inner GPS

Why might it be helpful to keep track of
your periods on a calendar?

NOW THAT YOU ARE A TEEN any doctor you see for a check-up or if you have been sick, will ask you, "When was your last period?" Having this information ready for your doctor helps her have a better understanding of your health.

ANOTHER REALLY GOOD REASON TO KEEP TRACK is that having an idea about the timing of your next period can help you avoid that "Uh oh, I just got my period!" moment. It's not so much fun when it happens at school.

IF YOUR PERIOD SNEAKS UP ON YOU

and you are away from home and need some help, you can ask any woman. She's been there, too.

AT SCHOOL YOU CAN TELL YOUR TEACHER

or go to the school nurse. You know what? Your male teachers or any school staff should be kind and understanding, too. That's part of their job!

PACKED AND READY

It's a good idea to keep a period kit in your backpack or purse. Many pharmacies and online sources sell them. We love one that comes with a mini heating pad!

IT'S EASY TO MAKE A KIT YOURSELF

by using a zip top bag or pouch. Just add a couple of pads or tampons and anything else you may find helpful. (A little piece of candy would be ok.)

TRY TO BE PREPARED

for every doctor appointment, and at school, and **KNOW YOUR CYCLE or KYC**.

WE'LL SHOW YOU HOW!

Grab a calendar off the wall, the Internet, or make one yourself.

THE FIRST DAY OF YOUR PERIOD

is considered to be the first day of your menstrual cycle.

SO, WE COUNT

from the first day of our periods to figure out when the next one will start.

MARK THE CALENDAR ON THE FIRST DAY OF YOUR PERIOD

with a symbol like a crown – or a flower – whatever makes you happy. Add your little symbol to the calendar each day of your period, including the last day when you may only see a little bit of blood.

Then **COUNT 24-31** days from the **FIRST** day of your period, to see when you will most likely have it again.

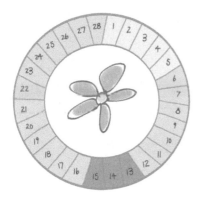

Many grown women use a circular menstrual cycle tracker to help them determine when they will have a period.

TRACKER APPS AND WEBSITES are a fun and helpful way to stay on track. You can track privately or track in tandem, a.k.a. together, with your friends!

IT CAN TAKE A LITTLE TIME TO GET YOUR OWN PERSONAL RHYTHM but eventually you will discover how many days your period will last, and how many days between each period.

Did you know that you and your BFFs can cycle at the same time, like at camp? So strange!

Hormonal Mischief

Sweet Sour Salty Fruity

REMEMBER THE HORMONES FROM OUR OVULATION FAIRY TALE?

Well, they are very real! The simplest explanation is that hormones are **NATURAL CHEMICALS** in your body. They are usually "made" in one part and travel to another part, to help your various systems function (like your reproductive system). Sometimes, the side effects of these traveling hormones can make you feel a little weird.

While waiting for your period to start, some hormones can get a little fidgety and cause you to laugh at sad things, cry at funny ones – and sometimes do both at the same time. They could make your breasts feel like heavy watermelons, and your skin could pop up in pimples. (Horrors!)

AND, HUNGRY?

You bet! All you want are the seven dwarves of appetite-gone-wild: sweet, sour, salty, fruity, crunchy, chewy, munchy, and sticky – all at once.

OH, AND THERE'S MORE . . .

You can get really crabby, flipping out at your family and offending your friends!

Crunchy Chewy Munchy Sticky

DIARRHEA OR CONSTIPATION

is another just fabulous and common aspect of hormonal monkey business right before and during your period. It will pass.

GOOD NEWS!

All of these pesky symptoms put together are known as **PREMENSTRUAL SYNDROME (PMS)**. And, there are things in your control to help you help yourself be emotionally, mentally, and physically in balance during this crazy little period before each period.

PMS IS A GREAT REASON TO KYC!

When you have a disagreement with your pets or say something mean to someone you love, it can be such a relief to look at the calendar and discover you are about to get your period.

If you experience a little PMS from time to time, you are completely normal.

HORMONAL = NORMONAL

Hormonal Rollercoaster

The two hormones you may have heard the most about are **ESTROGEN (EST-ro-jen)** and **PROGESTERONE (pro-JEST-er-own)**. Their movement throughout your pelvic region is pretty noticeable. Let's take a look at how these hormones can affect your energy and moods over the course of a month:

WEEK 1 You get your period. The great news about getting your period is that estrogen rises (it's nearly gone right before your period), and your mood may change from sad and cranky to chatty, bubbly, and sunny. What a perfect reason to appreciate your period! If you felt pooped heading into your period, you're now likely to feel pretty spunky.

WEEK 2 Estrogen continues to rise and you feel good. You may even feel more beautiful! Your world becomes all kittens and puppies and rainbows. Your optimism and motivation are revved up and ready. From an energy standpoint, you're super quick and super sharp, making walking, talking, texting, even testing fast and fun. You are ready, Freddie.

146

WEEK 3 Right around now, the Princess of Ovulation makes her move. Your hormones work their magic making it possible for her to scoot on out of your ovary. Your moods this week? Well, you could be a little weepy, and a little sleepy. Won't it be helpful to know about this stuff when things don't seem quite right? You can say to yourself, "No WONder!"

WEEK 4 Here's the week that lots of girls and women dread. You don't have to, though! Your hormones this week dip to their lowest point before you get your period, and the PMS fun begins. Ok, here we go: constipation (remember your fiber, water, and exercise); cramps (we'll get to those in a minute); bloating (again – water and exercise); feeling like you are slogging through mud; riding the roller coaster of grumpy to giddy and back again; and sleepy - but don't go hibernating. Believe us, when you feel low, exercise lifts you right back up.

Now check out Week 1 again to see the clouds parting!

WEEK 3

WEEK 4

WEEK 1

THAT'S YOUR MONTHLY RUN DOWN

Whenever in doubt, track your periods, and look back at our energy and mood guide to help you figure out where you may be in your cycle.

Cramps Cramp Your Style

WE ARE GOING TO TALK ABOUT CRAMPS
more than you thought possible because cramps happen!

GENTLE PELVIC CONTRACTIONS
squeeze out blood and lining, usually right before and for the first day or so of your period. Sometimes this activity isn't so gentle, and some lucky girls don't feel much at all.

IF YOU SUFFER
from really painful cramping, you might feel so tired that you can only sit in the dark or sleep. We know it feels awful, but try your best to keep moving. Hard to believe, but it's actually the best remedy.

IT'S ALL GOOD
LET IT GO – LET IT FLOW
Your grown-up can give you an over-the-counter pain reliever if absolutely necessary, but try to get very calm and change your frame of mind.

DON'T LET PMS OR CRAMPS GET THE BEST OF YOU!
Try to be mindful that they will most likely pass in a few days. Here are some tips to help you manage the mayhem.

RESIST THE URGE TO CURL UP IN A BALL

It may seem like a good idea, but doing it will just make you think about your cramps more. **PLEASE GO TO SCHOOL.** Participate in gym class and your after-school activities. Being busy is better. Being around friends is best.

A HEATING PAD WORKS WELL

Look for the kind you can stick right where the pain is, and avoid the plug-in kind.

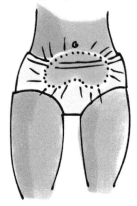

MOVIN' AND GROOVIN'

Movement helps to circulate blood through your body and release the nice, "good mood" hormones known as **ENDORPHINS (en-DOR-fins)**.

EAT FRESH FRUITS AND VEGGIES
Just do it!

DRINK WATER

The content of your body is largely water, so drinking it and keeping your body-water balance in check is crucial. Bloating is a normal part of having a period, and though it may seem like the opposite thing to do when your body is hanging on to fluids, it's true that water will help flush it out!

TAP INTO YOUR INNER YOGI

to boost your mood and relieve body aches. See the next pages for two helpful poses.

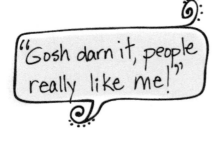

AFFIRM YOUR WONDERFULNESS

Remember, how you think can greatly affect how you feel.

Celery eases bloating and almonds are high in non-dairy calcium which can relax your muscles and ease your cramps.

SPEND TIME IN NATURE

Studies have shown that the colors and sounds outdoors along with fresh air can improve your mood. If you are a city girl, even a visit to the park can spark good feelings. Go ahead and hug that tree.

EAT A LITTLE CHOCOLATE!

A small amount of dark chocolate with over 70% cocoa can relax your muscles and ease your cramps.

The point is, take your mind off of pesky symptoms. You want to do something that makes you feel better without leaving your daily responsibilities behind.

IF THAT MEANS FORAGING for some heavier foods, like a cheeseburger, fries, and a shake, go for it – but don't overdo it – it's not a permission slip to overindulge. Also, if you feel like taking a nap after school, that's ok too.

Helpful Yoga Poses for Cramps

IF MENSTRUAL CRAMPS ARE BRINGING YOU DOWN TRY THESE YOGA POSES TO RELIEVE THE PAIN AND LIFT YOUR MOOD.

HEAD-TO-KNEE FORWARD BENDS

1. Sit on the floor with your legs extended in front of you.

2. With a TVA hug and an elongated spine, bend your left knee so that the bottom of your left foot lies against your right inner thigh, creating a triangle.

3. Now, exhale and gently stretch over your right leg, and reach for your toes.

4. As you stretch over your right leg, hang on to that TVA hug and try to make your spine as long as possible.

5. Hold for a count of 10 Mississippi's or more. Switch legs, and you're done!

If you can't quite reach those toes yet, no worries. The more often you stretch, the closer to your toes you'll get.

PELVIC BRIDGES

1 Lie on your back with your legs outstretched on the floor and your arms by your sides.

2 Slide your heels toward your tush so that your knees are directly above your ankles.

3 Make sure your feet are flat on the floor and hip width apart.

4 Push down on your heels and lift your butt off the ground. Press your shoulder blades into the floor.

5 Take three deep breaths in this pose then lower your butt back to the ground, vertebra by vertebra. (Remember that bicycle chain from Chapter 6?)

Yoga is meant to relax you, so don't speed-pose. Go slowly, and breathe fully.

THOUGH RARE
some girls may experience extra-heavy cramping and bleeding, making it very hard to keep a normal day-to-day routine.

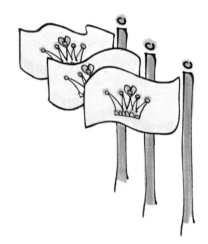

IF YOUR MOODS BLOW LIKE FLAGS
in gale force winds or your cramps are too hard to bear each time you have a period, it's time to see your doctor. You could be diagnosed with something more severe than PMS, and she or he can prescribe medication and share ideas for managing your symptoms.

The Magic Pelvis in Pregnancy

WHILE A WOMAN IS PREGNANT
she will not get her monthly period because the endometrial lining and iron-rich blood of her uterus actually nourish the growing baby inside.

IT'S PRETTY AMAZING that a whole new life grows within the uterus (cool doctor words: *in utero*) for nine months. A woman's uterus stretches to fit and protect her growing child, and then shrinks back down to original size in no time flat.

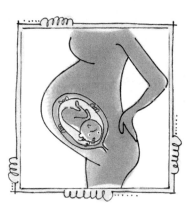

Why do pregnant women feel queezy? Those crazy court jester hormones create morning sickness!

HERE' SOMETHING TO THINK ABOUT: Could you imagine just showing up one day to run the Boston Marathon?

NINE MONTHS OF PREGNANCY is a little like a Pelvic Boston Marathon, and the muscles requiring the most training are the . . . wait for it . . . PFM!!

...WHILE THE CALM AND CLEVER HORMONES kick into action relaxing muscles, softening the cervix and other parts of the pelvis, helping the body get ready for delivery.

NO WAY! You would train to get into shape, learn how to sprint, practice going the distance, and prepare for recovery.

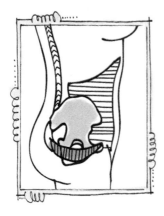

YOU LEARNED THAT PFM are pretty important when it comes to bladder and bowel health. They actually play their biggest role in pregnancy.

Perry Who?

We have talked about how many years a woman will have a period. Another milestone in a woman's life is when she nears the end of her reproductive years, the end of her periods.

The name for this phase is **PERIMENOPAUSE**, and then, when it's all over and done with, usually around the age of 50, it's called **MENOPAUSE**.

You go through many hormonal changes each month when you get your period; especially the one leading up to your first one.

WHEN A WOMAN EXPERIENCES PERIMENOPAUSE she goes through a **WHOLE NEW SET OF CHANGES**. She may experience insomnia (a hard time falling or staying asleep), "hot flashes," forgetfulness, and she could become a wee bit grumpy.

Be nice to your mama (or another woman you know) when it seems she's a little off her game, and don't be afraid to ask her about it. Try to give a little extra TLC (tender loving care). She's been there through all of your changes; now it's your turn to be patient with her! Beginning, middle or end of the reproductive process: It all happens in your enchanted and miraculous pelvic region. Now, let's go find out about keeping that area below your belt sparkly clean.

CHAPTER NINE

How to Be a Clean Queen

KEEPING CLEAN BELOW YOUR BELT

is a pretty easy thing to do. It's important, too. Not tending to cleanliness – having poor hygiene – can lead to infection and odors from your pelvic region. In the last chapter you learned that your body has its own natural cleansing mechanisms, like periods. Some parts of your body need to be cleaned and looked after by you. This includes your "outside" pelvic parts.

What Does Clean Mean?

DO YOU KNOW THE RHYME THAT STARTS WITH "GIRLS ARE MADE OF . . . ?"

Girls are made of sugar and spice and everything nice.
Boys are made of snakes and snails and puppy dog tails.

SO, BASICALLY BOYS

like to get dirty and play with "boy" things, and girls are sweet and lovely and sit still? That may be cute, but these well-loved words also suggest that it's ok for boys to sweat and smell, but girls should not.

WELL, THAT'S NOT TRUE

Some girls love to get muddy and look for bugs, or play basketball, or go running, or become archeologists or professional athletes.

The sweaty, dirty stuff is not only for boys, and it's ok to smell!

**WE KNOW IT CAN BE
A CHALLENGE**

to grow up in a culture where you are bombarded with advertisements on TV and the Internet stating you should be, feel, and smell as clean as a breeze on a lake.

YOU ARE SHOWN IMAGES which suggest you are not clean unless you use deodorant sprays and other products inside and around your vagina!

**WELL, WE URGE YOU
NOT TO BELIEVE IT,
AND HERE'S WHY**

A girl's body, just like a boy's, has its own natural, healthy odors. Covering up these nature-made smells with perfumes, powders, and sprays can actually cause unwanted bacteria to grow and create more odors, which can be truly unpleasant.

A good friend of ours says, "Roses over funky smells just make rosy, funky smells."

IF SMELLING WORSE

is not enough to keep you away from the stuff, just know most of these so-called good-for-you products can cause **INFECTION** and **IRRITATION**, which means you need more products to make them go away.

LOTS OF GIRLS AND WOMEN fall into this never-ending cycle: Spray. Smell. Spray. Smell. Spray. You get the picture.

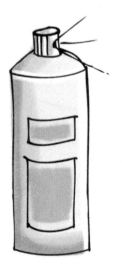

PLEASE DON'T LET ANYONE tell you that you need to use a spray or a powder for your vaginal area. She, he or they would be **WRONG**.

Don't always believe what you see or hear.

JUST BECAUSE A PRODUCT EXISTS doesn't mean you have to use it, and doesn't mean it's good for you. There's nothing like a pretty box or bottle to hypnotize you into buying it. Resist!

Sometimes odors from sweat can linger on your clothes even after washing. If you are not doing the laundry yourself these days, let your grown-up know that adding half a cup of vinegar to the washing machine will zap odors, leaving your favorite gym shorts and t-shirts super fresh – with no added chemicals.

Rockin' Your Pelvic Hygiene

Ok, this is like the shortest section of the whole book:

WHEN IT COMES TO HYGIENE
our recommendation is that you simply use warm water to clean the area of your vulva, your labia majora and minora, and around the opening of your vagina.

THAT'S IT!
Your healthy vagina is like a self-cleaning oven. It takes care of itself.

Back in Chapter 6 you learned that K.I.S.S. means
"KEEP IT STRONG, SISTER!"

Well, K.I.S.S. also stands for
"KEEP IT SIMPLE, SWEETIE!"

YOU CAN USE VERY MILD, PH-BALANCED SOAP

on the outside areas where you may have pubic hair and around your anus and **PERINEUM (peri-NEE-um).**

EVEN WHEN YOU HAVE YOUR PERIOD

or you've gotten really sweaty, a clean washcloth and warm water will do the trick. (You aren't rubbing out a spot, so be gentle with yourself, too!) Keep it simple and pure, and you can be confident in your cleanliness.

TRY TO AVOID

heavily scented, harsh soaps especially around your labia majora and minora.

And, for goodness sake, stay away from bubble bath. You'll take a trip straight to **ITCHY TOWN**.

PERINEUM

We haven't actually talked about this special part of your anatomy. It's that random piece of real estate between your vagina and your anus. Though it may seem kind of awkward, this area actually has a job. During pregnancy and delivery, the perineum stretches to make room for a baby's head to pass through the vaginal opening.

What Can Go Wrong Even When You Do Things Right

WHEN YOU DO THINGS JUST AS YOU HAVE BEEN TOLD like brushing your teeth to prevent cavities or studying for a test in order to get a good grade, you expect things to go as planned, but they don't always.

THE SAME GOES FOR PELVIC HEALTH You can have the best bathroom behaviors, eat and drink the right foods, be queenly clean, and still stuff comes up.

Odors and Colors and Discharge, Oh My!

JUST AS YOUR PERIOD BLOOD is different than blood from a cut, your natural body odors and sweaty smells are different than odors from vaginal irritation or infection.

IF YOU PAY ATTENTION it's not that hard to figure out which ones are fine, and which ones may be unhealthy.

DISCHARGE IS ONE OF THOSE WORDS you're either fine with or it makes you shudder. The plain truth is it just means "that which is expelled or pushed out" – in this case, from your body. Pimple gunk is discharged, for instance.

BELOW YOUR BELT, DISCHARGE CAN BE HEALTHY
like Cervical Fluid - or unhealthy as with infection or irritation.

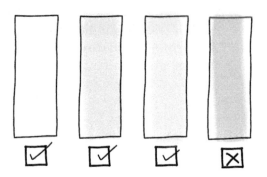

NOTICE YOUR BODY'S NORMAL FLUIDS, COLORS, AND ODORS

If something looks or feels different, has an unusually strong or unpleasant odor, or if you have clumpy or off-color discharge, you most likely have some kind of fixable, treatable infection or irritation. Phew!

IT'S FAIR TO SAY IF IT'S DIFFERENT THAN WHAT YOU EXPECT

and there's a mild gross-out factor to go along with it, then it's time to see the doctor.

UTIs and Something New: Vaginal Yeast Infections

MOST GIRLS AND WOMEN

at some time in their life experience the joys of a Urinary Tract Infection (UTI) or a Vaginal Yeast Infection (VYI). We talked about UTIs in Chapter 3 so you already know a little about them, but what about these yeast infections?

YEAST IS A COMPLICATED little fungus found in nature, in food, in the air, and in your body. Some yeasts are good, some are harmful. The kind of yeast found in and on various parts of your body can go either way.

YEAST SHARES THE SPACE in your vagina with bacteria, some good, some bad. Sometimes, bacteria can outgrow the yeast creating a bacterial infection, and more often, yeast can outgrow the bacteria, upsetting the fine balance, and causing infections or "flare-ups."

A VYI CAUSES IRRITATION and is usually crazy itchy, and most often produces vaginal discharge, literally the overgrowth of yeast which you can actually see. Lovely.

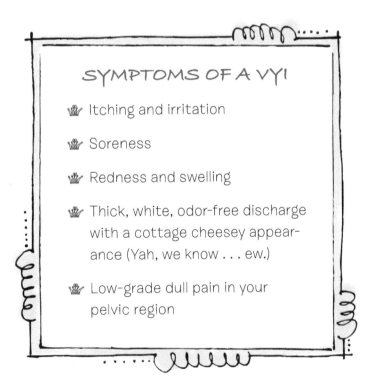

SYMPTOMS OF A VYI

- 👑 Itching and irritation

- 👑 Soreness

- 👑 Redness and swelling

- 👑 Thick, white, odor-free discharge with a cottage cheesey appearance (Yah, we know . . . ew.)

- 👑 Low-grade dull pain in your pelvic region

HOW TO AVOID A VYI

👑 Change your bathing suit as soon as you are finished swimming - yeast loves moisture.

👑 Change your underpants after you exercise – not only does yeast love moisture, it especially likes *warm*, wet places.

👑 Sleep WITHOUT your underpants (unless you have your period) - nightgowns were invented to cover you up and air you out.

👑 Wear cotton underpants, especially if you are prone to yeast infections. Silky, stretchy panties may be tempting, but cotton is a natural material which allows the moisture from your vagina to dry up and disappear.

👑 Avoid those perfumes and heavily scented soaps – as we have pointed out, they can irritate and actually cause yeast to grow.

👑 Think about eating less sugar – yeast grows and multiplies when you gobble up the sweet stuff.

👑 If a doctor prescribes an antibiotic when you are sick, also ask for a probiotic. Antibiotics destroy both bad and good bacteria in the body. Probiotics help replace the good stuff, which then helps keep yeast in balance.

UTIs ARE COMMON BUT NOT NORMAL

You may remember from Chapter 3 that girls and women are more susceptible to UTIs than boys and men because of their body structure. Bacteria can spread from your anus to your urethra because they are so close together. That's why we wipe from front to back.

Heavily scented sprays and soaps are also responsible for many a UTI.

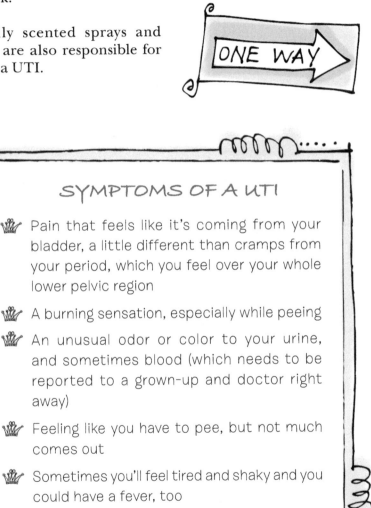

SYMPTOMS OF A UTI

- Pain that feels like it's coming from your bladder, a little different than cramps from your period, which you feel over your whole lower pelvic region

- A burning sensation, especially while peeing

- An unusual odor or color to your urine, and sometimes blood (which needs to be reported to a grown-up and doctor right away)

- Feeling like you have to pee, but not much comes out

- Sometimes you'll feel tired and shaky and you could have a fever, too

YOUR DOCTOR WILL PRESCRIBE CREAM OR OINTMENT or tablets if you have a VYI, and an antibiotic for a UTI. Never take non-prescription medication without your doctor's permission.

A FRIENDLY REMINDER:

- Step **AWAY** from the vagina spray!
- Keep the clean routine simple and pure.
- Get help when you have any VYI or UTI symptoms.

You are so informed at this point. Are you feeling a closer connection to your pelvic region, like you rule the school, drive the bus, wield the staff, wear the crown? If you said, "Yes!" you are on your way to becoming . . .

(Drum roll, trumpets, and glitter, please!)

CHAPTER TEN:
Large and in Charge as Queen of your Pelvic Region!

TA DA! YOU MADE IT THROUGH QUEEN TRAINING

You know more about your pelvic region now than many girls and women will ever know over the course of their whole life - unless you start spreading the news! Before you close the book, we have some final, friendly thoughts as you head into the rest of your healthy life.

Decisions, Decisions

YOU HAVE SO MANY CHOICES THESE DAYS, MORE THAN ANY GENERATION BEFORE YOU
Whether TV, Internet, friends or family, you've got information coming at you from all angles. Having a choice can be good, and it can sometimes make things confusing.

JUST REMEMBER, EVERYONE IS DIFFERENT
What may work or be true for your BFF may not be the case for you. Find what brings out your best, and stick with what is working already. Trust your instincts, and repeat after us: "In me, I trust!"

BEING INFORMED AND EDUCATED
about yourself and your world, can make decision making much easier. That's true for all kinds of choices you may have to make in life.

**YOUR GROWN-UPS
DO THEIR BEST**
to keep you healthy and teach you how to take care of yourself. You can help them by becoming aware of how your body works, and communicate with them when you think something isn't right.

LEARN HOW TO RECOGNIZE and share when you feel strong, energetic, happy, and healthy, too. This is a wonderful way to "be" and is often brought about by making good choices!

Being prepared, informed, and responsible may sound like a bunch of mumbo jumbo now, but you'll need to be all of that to remain safe and healthy when it comes to sexual activity. Yes, we said the "S" word! A good example is the **HUMAN PAPILLOMA VIRUS (HPV)** vaccine. Your doctor may already have suggested that you become vaccinated. HPV is passed on by unsafe sexual activity and can lead to cancer of the cervix. There's no shame in learning more by talking to your doctor about it, and doing so is a brilliant move in the direction of smart decision making!

Your Pelvic Health, Your Life

AS QUEEN OF YOUR PELVIC REGION
it makes sense that you will have choices to make about your pelvic health in particular.

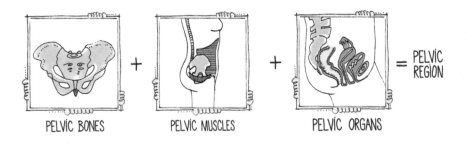

PELVIC BONES   +   PELVIC MUSCLES   +   PELVIC ORGANS   =   PELVIC REGION

IT MAY BE HARD TO MAKE THE CONNECTION
or imagine that choices you make and habits you have now, can affect your health and happiness as you grow and get older, but ignoring or pushing your pelvic health aside is not the healthiest one.

Here are some small decisions you might make today that could lead to very positive outcomes in the future.

HYGIENE
Don't use feminine sprays.

EXERCISE
Have a daily dose of Pelvic Pyramid exercise.

NUTRITION
Help your bladder be gladder and your bowels behave.

PRACTICES
Remember the Potty Pledge.

NO DOUBT, YOU'VE HEARD

that the knee bone is connected to the thigh bone. Well, many of the major systems in your body are connected to your pelvis. If being happy is important to you, then actively pursuing good pelvic health matters.

Practice Makes Perfect

**WINNING YOUR NEXT
SOCCER GAME**
or performing for an audience
or going to Mars: When you
have a dream, sometimes it's all
you can think about. If you are
ill or weakened in any way, it
can be much more challenging
to maintain your focus.

**AS YOU HAVE PROBABLY
FIGURED OUT**
the more you choose to
practice anything – a musical
instrument, a new language,
your favorite sport, the better
you get at that activity. The
better you get, the greater the
end result.

**THE SAME GOES FOR THE
HEALTHY PELVIC LESSONS**
you have learned with us here.
Can you name the muscles and
bones of your Pelvic Region?
Could you tell your doctor
when your last period was?

IT'S SMART TO THINK ABOUT THESE THINGS
With familiarity and practice, you'll become quite the expert on
yourself.

Share the Health

WHEN YOU TAKE GOOD CARE OF YOURSELF
you experience personal growth. When you share your knowledge with others, you are participating in, and advancing something called **PUBLIC HEALTH** – health which affects a greater number of people, right now and in the future. So, in a small way, you wind up making the world a healthier, happier place, one person – or pelvis – at a time.

What does a queen know about the region she rules?

WELL, AS YOU THINK ABOUT EACH CHAPTER OF *BELOW YOUR BELT*, DOES ANY OF THIS SOUND FAMILIAR?

- She knows the history and culture of her region.

- She knows the boundaries and the geography of her territories.

- She knows her region's engineering – how and why things work.

- She knows how to keep her region strong, what it needs to thrive and flourish.

- She knows her region's sensitivities, places that will need some special attention and care, both now and in the future.

- And, she knows how to be a leader and rule the region, feeling worthy of her job and her title, and completely in charge.

THAT'S YOU, YOUR HIGHNESS! REIGN OVER YOUR PELVIC REGION WITH CONFIDENCE AND PRIDE.

Am I Hydrated?

LET'S SEE, WHAT COLOR IS MY PEE?

This simple color chart can help you figure out if you are drinking enough fluids throughout the day to stay hydrated.

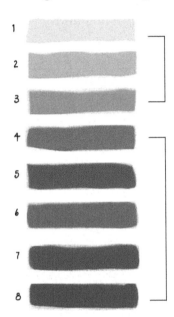

If your pee matches numbers 1 to 3, then you are hydrated.

If your urine looks more like numbers 4 to 8, then you may be dehydrated and need to drink a few more glasses of water each day to be in the pale yellow.

Sometimes strong vitamins can change the color of your urine for a few hours. If yours should happen to stay in the darker part of this range, and you are not taking vitamins, please let your grown-up know. Your doctor will probably want to make sure everything's working ok.

Do you know what Asparagus Pee is? Sometimes asparagus can make your pee smell wicked weird. If you haven't had asparagus, and you have strong-smelling urine, it could also be a sign that you are becoming dehydrated.

The Amazing Bristol Stool Chart

Does this chart shock you? It might. But it shouldn't. Remember, everybody poops – your parents, your classmates, your teachers - we just don't like to talk about it. This chart was created in the 1970s to classify the shape of poop into seven categories. It's a handy way to think about your poop because what it looks like can tell you and your doctor a lot about how fast your poop leaves your body, how you process different foods or about any illnesses you may have.

TYPE 1

TYPE 2

If you have to push to poop and it matches numbers 1 and 2, you are constipated!

TYPE 3

TYPE 4

If it glides right out and looks more like numbers 3 and 4, you're in great poop shape. Some people say if it makes you think of toothpaste, it's perfect.

TYPE 5

TYPE 6

If your poop can't actually hold its shape, you are heading into diarrhea land. Make sure you report it to your grown-up if it lasts more than a day.

TYPE 7

There are other stool charts that give you even *more* information like if your poop appears to be greasy or dry, stringy or thick, or gray, or brown, or black. Yuck and cool at the same time!

Fiber Finds!

Remember this helpful bit of math: The amount of fiber you need each day is based on the number 10 plus your age.

Check it out: If you happen to be 12 years old, you should try have $10 + 12 = 22$ grams of fiber to keep things moving smoothly. What we have listed here are foods high in fiber and easy to get at the store. Combine 'em for a boost!

FRUITS

Raspberries	Apples
Blackberries	Bananas
Avocados	Oranges
Plums (Prunes!)	Grapefruits
	Strawberries

VEGETABLES

Spinach	Collard Greens
Green Peas	Green Beans
Broccoli	Corn

GRAINS, CEREAL, PASTA

Whole Wheat Pasta	Muffins
Fiber cereal	Oatmeal
Oat Bran	Brown Rice

LEGUMES, NUTS, SEEDS

Lentils	Edamame (soy beans)
Black Beans	Sunflower Seeds
Garbanzo Beans	
	Almonds

SNACKS

Fruit Leather	Popcorn

A word of caution here is that lots of packaged foods say "High Fiber" or "High Protein," but make sure you read all the ingredients because many of these are also loaded with sugar – a whole other nutritional topic.

"Tell Me About It" Interview

Someone special in your life would probably be honored if you asked her a few questions about her own experiences with menstruation. A mom or a sister, a grandmother, an aunt, even a favorite teacher would have plenty to say to help you get an idea about how connected you are to other women in your life. Grab a notebook or journal, add some questions of your own, and off you go.

1. How old were you when you got your period?

2. How did you feel about it (excited, scared, etc.)?

3. Do you remember where you were?

4. Were you prepared for it – did your mom or someone tell you what to expect?

5. And, were you *prepared* for it – did you have any kind of pad with you in your purse?

6. Who did you tell first or did you keep it a secret?

7. Did you ever stop activities on the days you had your period? Why?

8. Did you ever feel ashamed about having your period?

9. What did you wish you had known about periods when you were younger?

10. Do you have any advice about periods you would be willing to share with me?

Girls' Talk to Dads

Sometimes talking to a man about your body can be a little awkward. We wish it weren't so, but it just is. You may be able to shift that feeling to the positive side by practicing what you have learned here in BYB. What helps is knowing what to talk about, and talking about what you know!

Before you talk to the trusted man in your life about things going on below your belt, you may find it helpful to have a plan. Here are some ideas:

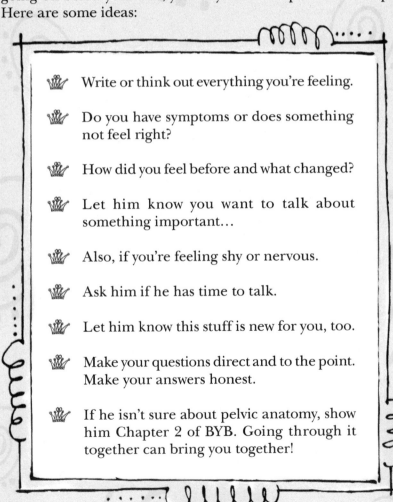

- 👑 Write or think out everything you're feeling.

- 👑 Do you have symptoms or does something not feel right?

- 👑 How did you feel before and what changed?

- 👑 Let him know you want to talk about something important…

- 👑 Also, if you're feeling shy or nervous.

- 👑 Ask him if he has time to talk.

- 👑 Let him know this stuff is new for you, too.

- 👑 Make your questions direct and to the point. Make your answers honest.

- 👑 If he isn't sure about pelvic anatomy, show him Chapter 2 of BYB. Going through it together can bring you together!

Dads' Talk to Girls

Dads – You may have no idea the impact you have on your girls. From year one to year twenty-one, you are likely to have close contact with this beauty of yours. And of course, the messages you give your daughter through your actions will have the greatest impact during these years. You have the opportunity to gain her implicit trust by being interested in what interests her and perceptive and compassionate when she appears to need your help. Part of that interaction is going to involve her health, in particular her pelvic health. Menstruation, mood swings, hygiene, and fitness are all things you may feel a little unprepared to discuss, but please take the opportunity to do so. It can set the stage for positive interaction with men as she heads into the different stages of her adult life. There are many books and resources out there. You can start with this one, and you can build from the ideas listed on the previous page.

Ask questions; listen; and help her feel she has done the right thing by sharing her concerns – or triumphs – with you.

Whether father, extended family, or trusted member of the community, your role in a girl's life is a gift to you. Rest assured that sensitive guidance – and a little humor – go a long way.

Text It!

BYB Below Your Belt

CF Cervical Fun. See Cervical Fluid.

JICP Just-in-Case Peeing

KISS Keep It Strong, Sister
or Keep It Simple, Sweetie

KYC Know Your Cycle. The first day of your
menstrual cycle is first day you see blood.

LBL Little Bitty Leaks.
See Light bladder Leakage.

MM Mighty Muscle. See Multifidus.

PFM Pretty Fabulous Muscles.
See Pelvic Floor Muscles.

TLC Tender Loving Care

TVA See Transverse Abdominal.

UTI See Urinary Tract Infection.

VYI See Vaginal Yeast Infection.

Glossary

Abdomen the part of your body you think of as your middle, belly or stomach. The upper parts of the small and large intestines are found here and in the pelvic region.

Appendix A tiny pocket-shaped organ that sits between your small and large intestines. Some scientists think that healthy gut bacteria hang out here and come to the rescue when you have an infection anywhere in your digestive tract. Appendicitis is when your appendix becomes inflamed. An Appendectomy is the surgery that removes it from your body. No worries! People get along just fine without an appendix.

Antibiotic A medicine that stops the growth of or destroys bacteria and other microorganisms.

Anus The opening in your pelvic region at the end of the digestive tract where solid waste (poop) leaves your body.

Bladder A muscular organ that stores urine.

Bowel Movement When solid waste leaves the body through the anus. AKA pooping.

Cervical Fluid Mucus secreted by the cervix. Cervical fluid changes in consistency throughout a woman's menstrual cycle.

Cervix A cylinder-shaped tunnel of tissue that connects the vagina and uterus. If you were to view the cervix straight on, it would look a little like a doughnut.

Clitoris A pea-sized organ, located where the labia majora and vagina come together, just below the mons pubis. It is very sensitive to the touch and covered by skin which acts like a hood to protect it.

Coccyx A small, triangular bone at the base of the spinal column, just below the sacrum. Frequently referred to as the tail bone.

Colon Another name for large intestine.

Constipation When bowel movements become difficult or less frequent.

Digestion The process of breaking down food once it is eaten. After passing through the stomach digested food continues to move through the intestines.

Elimination The process of expelling or removing waste from the body.

Endometrium The inner lining of the uterus which is shed during menstruation.

Endorphins Hormones that work to block the feeling of pain.

Fallopian Tubes The pair of tubes that carries an ovum from the ovary to the uterus.

Feces/Fecal Matter Waste that leaves the body through the anus.

Fiber The material in some plants that cannot be fully digested. An important part of your nutrition, fiber helps push other foods through your intestines so you don't become constipated.

Frequency In regard to urination, the "always have to go" feeling.

Genitals/Genitalia External reproductive organs, "private parts."

Gland Small organs throughout the body that hold on to or release substances to other parts of the body. Ovaries are considered glands.

Gynecology The branch of medicine that focuses on the pelvic health of women and girls, especially of the reproductive system. The doctor who practices this branch of medicine is known as a Gynecologist.

Hormones Natural chemical substances that circulate through the blood stream and influence various systems such as digestion, metabolism, menstruation, growth, reproduction, and moods.

Human Papilloma Virus (HPV) An infection that can cause warts or live in the bloodstream. There are many types of harmless warts, but some, which are found on the genitals, often lead to cervical (cervix) and some other cancers if left untreated. Because genital HPV is passed on during sexual activity, both tween and teen girls and boys may receive an HPV vaccine provided by a pediatrician or family doctor, to protect them during their adult years.

Hygiene The things that you do to keep yourself and the space around you clean in order to maintain good health.

Incontinence The loss of control or inability to stop urine or feces from leaving the body.

JIC-Peeing Using the bathroom before you actually need to, "just in case..."

Kidneys A pair of organs that filters waste from your blood and body as urine.

Labia Majora and Minora The outer and inner lips of the vulva, formed by folds of soft skin.

Large Intestine The lower portion of the intestines, connected to the small intestine on one end, and the rectum at the other end.

Light Bladder Leakage (LBL) Losing a little bit of urine when you laugh, cough, sneeze or during sports.

Menarche When a female menstruates for the first time.

Menopause The point in a woman's life when she has not had her period for one year and marks the end of childbearing years.

Menses The monthly flow of blood and the endometrial lining from the uterus through the vagina. Another name for menstruation.

Menstrual Cycle The number of days between periods, typically 26 – 32 days. The cycle includes ovulation and your period. The first day of a period is considered to be the first day of the cycle.

Mons Pubis The rounded fleshy padding over the pubic bone that becomes covered with hair during puberty.

Multifidus A muscle that runs deep along the spine. Your Multifidus creates the back of the Pelvic Pyramid.

Obstetrics The branch of medicine related to childbirth. Many gynecologists are also obstetricians, and are referred to as "OBGYNs."

Ovaries Two almond-sized "purses" or glands containing millions of eggs, also known as "ova."

Ovulation Part of the menstrual cycle when an ovary releases an egg, "ovum," to travel down the Fallopian tube where it is shed monthly, unless a woman becomes pregnant.

Pelvic Bones The two large bones that create the butterfly shape of the pelvis.

Pelvic Region The area between the abdomen and legs containing the bones, muscles, and organs of digestion, elimination, and reproduction.

Pelvic Floor Muscles (PFM) A group of muscles and ligaments that support the organs of the pelvis. Your PFM create the base of the Pelvic Pyramid.

Pelvic Pyramid The pelvic floor muscles, Transverse Abdominal, and Multifidus. They stabilize and support the pelvis, posture, and bladder and bowel control.

Perimenopause The stage in a women's life before menopause when she nears the end of her reproductive years.

Perineum The area between the anus and the vulva.

Physical Therapy The healthcare practice of working with patients who have pain or limited ability to walk or move. Pelvic Floor Physical Therapists help people with incontinence or pain in the pelvic region.

Premenstrual Syndrome (PMS) A wide range of physical and emotional symptoms caused by hormonal changes the days before you start your period.

Puberty When your reproductive organs become "activated," creating the start of periods, the growth of pubic hair, and many other hormonal changes in the body.

Pubic Bones Narrower bones which create the front of the pelvis, held together by the Pubic Symphysis.

Public Health The science of protecting and improving the health of individuals and communities through education and the promotion of healthy decisions.

Rectum The lowest section of the large intestine leading to the anus.

Reproductive System Includes the organs directly involved in producing eggs and in conceiving and carrying babies. Also known as sexual organs.

Small Intestine The winding, narrow, upper part of the intestine where digestion continues after food leaves the stomach and nutrients are absorbed. It is between the stomach and large intestine.

Taboo An experience or subject that people may find offensive or very difficult to talk about, for instance, various aspects of pelvic health.

Toxic Shock Syndrome A rare but serious infection caused by bacteria that enters the bloodstream. It occurs most commonly when synthetic tampons are worn longer than what is indicated in the tampon-use instructions.

Transverse Abdominal A deep abdominal muscle which wraps around your torso like a corset. Your TVA creates the front of the Pelvic Pyramid.

Ureters Thick tubes which take urine from the kidneys to the bladder.

Urethra A small tube which carries urine from the bladder to the toilet. The urethra is one of the three openings in a girl's pelvic region.

Urgency In regard to urination, the "gotta go right now" feeling.

Urine Pee. Yellowish fluid consisting of excess water, salt, and other waste substances.

Urogynecology The study of medicine devoted to repairing women's pelvic floor disorders such as bladder or bowel leakage. The doctor who practices this branch of medicine is known as a Urogynecologist.

Urinary Tract Infection (UTI) An infection found along the urinary tract. One type of UTI is a bladder infection.

Uterus A pear-shaped, hollow, muscular organ that stretches to hold a developing and growing baby.

Vagina The muscular passage leading from the cervix to the vulva. Menstrual blood passes through the vagina, as does a baby during childbirth.

Vulva The area that surrounds your vagina including the external female genitals.

Vaginal Yeast Infection An overgrowth of yeast characterized by itching, burning, soreness, and lumpy white discharge.

All Sorts of Resources

CHAPTER 1:
- *Below Your Belt online, belowyourbelt.org*
- *Museum of Menstruation and Women's Health, www.mum.org*
- *Women's Health Foundation, womenshealthfoundation.org*

CHAPTER 2:
- *Human Body Visual Dictionary, DK Books, 1999*
- *The Human Body and How it Works by Gregory J. Stewart, Facts on File, 2009*
- *I Heart Guts - plushies and t-shirts - iheartguts.com*

CHAPTER 3:
- *Don't Flush: Lifting the Lid on the Science of Poo and Wee by Richard and Mary Platt, Kingfisher Publishing, 2012*
- *The Truth about Poop and Pee: All the Facts on the Ins and Outs of Bodily Functions by Susan E. Goodman, Puffin, 2014*
- *Sitting Pretty Toilet Seat Covers, found at most Container Stores*
- *Coleman Toilet Seat Covers, found at most Walmart Stores*

CHAPTER 4:
- *Everybody Poops by Taro Gomi, Kane/Miller Book Publishing, 2001*
- *Food & You by Dr. Lynda Madison, American Girl, 2008*
- *Teen nutrition: Kidshealth.org/teen/food_fitness/nutrition/fiber.html*
- *Squatty Potty Toilet Stool - squattypotty.com*

CHAPTER 6:
- *Yoga Exercises for Teens: Developing a Calmer Mind and a Stronger Body by Helen Puperhart, Hunter House, 2008*

CHAPTER 7:
- *Cycle Savvy by Toni Weschler, Harper Perennial, 2011*
- *Everything a Girls Needs to Know About Her Periods by Jane Feinmann*
- *Gotcha Covered!: Everything You Need To Know About Your Period by Lisa McGuinness, Chris Boral, Chronicle Books, 2008*
- *Female Empowerment Bracelet - feby.com*
- *Friendly Guide to Healthy Periods - menstrupedia.com*

CHAPTER 8:
- *The Care & Keeping of You 2: The Body Book for Older Girls by Cara Natterson, American Girl, 2013*
- *Below Your Belt Conversations - bybconversations.com*
- *Cycleharmony.com*
- *Dot Girl First Period Kit - dotgirlproducts.com*
- *Helloflo.com*
- *Reusable Pads and leak-free panties - lunapads.com*
- *Menstrual cup - divacup.com*
- *Cycle tracker App, Clue - Helloclue.com*
- *Cycle tracker website, My Monthly Cycles - mymonthlycycles.com*
- *Girlology – girlology.com*

CHAPTER 9:
- *Is This Normal: Answered by the Editors of the Care & Keeping of You by Michelle Watkins, American Girl, 2009*
- *stlouischildrens.org; Search "clean and nearly teen"*

CHAPTER 10:
- *Know Your Worth: 365 Inspirational Quotes, Tweets, and Posts for Teenage Girls by Shawn M. McBride*

FOR PARENTS:
- *American Academy of Pediatrics Caring For Your Teenager by Philip Bashe, Bantam, 2003*
- *Mother-Daughter Wisdom: Understanding the Crucial Link between Mothers, Daughters, and Health by Christiane Northrup M.D., Bantam, 2006*
- *Mothering and Daughtering: Keeping your bond Strong Through the Teen Years by Eliza and Sil Reynolds, Sounds True, 2013*
- *Information and advice from the American Academy of Pediatrics - Healthychildren.org*
- *PBS Parenting Resources - Pbs.org/parents/parenting/raising-girls*

HELP ALONG THE WAY:

BOOKS
- *American Medical Association Girl's Guide to Becoming a Teen by AMA, Kate Gruenwald, Amy Middleman, Jossey-Bass, 2006*
- *The Big Book of HELP!: Both of the Absolutely Indispensable Guides to Life for Girls by Nancy Holyoke, American Girl Library, 2004*
- *The Care & Keeping of You by Valorie Schaefer, American Girl, 2012*
- *Girl Files: All About Puberty and Growing Up by Jacqui Bailey, Wayland, 2012*
- *Girl to Girl: Honest Talk About Growing Up and Your Changing Body by Sarah O'Leary Burningham, 2013*
- *The Girls' Life Guide to Growing Up by Karen Bokram, 2012*
- *Girl Stuff: A Survival Guide to Growing Up by Margaret Blackstone and Elissa Harden, Chronicle Books, 2013*
- *Growing Up: It's a Girl Thing by Mavis Jukes, Knopf Books for Young Readers, 1998*
- *Our Bodies, Ourselves by Boston Women's Health Book Collective, Judy Norsigian, Touchstone, 2011*
- *Ready, Set, Grow: A What's Happening to My Body? Book for Younger Girls by Lynda Madaras, William Morrow Books, 2003*
- *Secret Girls' Business by Fay Angelo, Heather Anderson, Rose Stewart (special edition offered for girls with autism, disability, or communication disorders), Secret Girls' Business, 2003*
- *The Teenage Body Book by Kathy McCoy, et al., 2008*
- *The Girl's Life: Guide to Growing up by Selene Yeager, 2012*
- *The "What's Happening to My Body?" Book for Girls by Lynda Madaras, William Morrow Paperbacks, 2007*

ONLINE
- *Information on health for girls 10-16 - Girlshealth.gov*
- *Health question and answer Internet resource - Goaskalice.columbia.edu*
- *Information Resource for kids, teens, and parents - Teenshealth.org*
- *The Center for Young Women's Health - Youngwomenshealth.org*
- *Mother & Daughter Relationship advice - Motheringanddaughtering.com*

Missy Lavender

Founder and Executive Director of Women's Health Foundation, Missy believes EVERY woman and girl deserves better pelvic health, so she can be powerful, confident and in control. She lives in Chicago with her teenage son and daughter, of whom she is most proud, and their two canine monsters.

This book and the work I do is dedicated to all my gal pals, my gal fam, and my daughter, named after my grandmother. All these powerful women help keep me motivated to change the world, one pelvic floor at a time.

Jeni Donatelli Ihm

A health educator and fitness professional for more than 20 years, when asked what Jeni does for a living, she often replies that she is professionally confused! Always seeking to learn more, Jeni discovered Women's Health Foundation and soaked up the wealth of information surrounding pelvic health. Jeni lives in Chicago with her husband and children where they love to explore their great city.

For my children whom I love and cherish. To my husband Joe, you are both my supportive partner and my inspiration. I watch you in awe, and you keep me moving. Thank you for being there for me, I love you.

Jan Dolby

Jan Dolby is the illustrator of the *Gabby* picture book series, *The Sugar Plum Tree*, and *Riding the Potty Train*. She studied fine art and business at the University of Guelph before embarking on a career as a children's book illustrator. Jan's studio, The Pink Suitcase, is located north of Toronto, Canada, where she lives with her husband and two children.

For my lovely daughter, Georgia Mae.

Further Acknowledgements

Elizabeth Wood would like to thank WHF's creative and hard-working interns and volunteers, Elizabeth Fisher, Keira Ferguson, Mikaela McDermott, Elizabeth Christopher, Jaclyn Patulo, and Katy O'Dwyer; and calm, cool, creative designer Michelle Ganeles.

WOMEN'S HEALTH FOUNDATION exists to improve the pelvic health and wellness of women and girls by sponsoring research, developing educational initiatives, and promoting innovative programs for patients and communities. To that end, all proceeds from the sale of *Below Your Belt* support its work with adolescents.

Women's Health Foundation

CPSIA information can be obtained
at www.ICGtesting.com
Printed in the USA
LVOW05s1822131215
466507LV00006B/21/P

9 780996 535809